BENEDI
CULTIVAT
JOY, A
AT WORK

Lead Like a Monk

Anselm Grün

PARACLETE PRESS
Brewster, Massachusetts

First published in English by Paraclete Press, 2022

Lead Like a Monk: Benedict's Path to Cultivating Meaning, Joy, and Purpose at Work

978-1-64060-508-4

Copyright © 2018 by Vier-Tuerme GmbH-Verlag

Translated from German by Peter Dahm Robertson: Anselm Grün, *Menschen führen: Leben wecken. Anregungen aus der Regel Benedikts von Nursia* ISBN 978-3-87868-132-8 © Vier-Türme GmbH, Verlag, Münsterschwarzach 1998 Alle Rechte vorbehalten.

Library of Congress Cataloging-in-Publication Data
Names: Grün, Anselm, author.
Title: Lead Like a Monk : Benedict's path to cultivating meaning, joy, and purpose at work / Anselm Grün.
Other titles: Menschen führen. English
Description: Brewster, Massachusetts : Paraclete Press, 2022. | Includes bibliographical references. | Summary: "The very practical aspects of leadership are explored: qualities of a leader, the handling of material possessions, self-care, relationships with others, and goals in leadership"-- Provided by publisher.
Identifiers: LCCN 2022002223 (print) | LCCN 2022002224 (ebook) | ISBN 9781640605084 | ISBN 9781640605091 (epub) | ISBN 9781640605107 (pdf)
Subjects: LCSH: Leadership--Religious aspects--Christianity. | Benedict, Saint, Abbot of Monte Cassino. Regula. | BISAC: RELIGION / Christian Living / Spiritual Growth
Classification: LCC BV4597.53.L43 G7813 2022 (print) | LCC BV4597.53.L43 (ebook) | DDC 248.8/8--dc23/eng/20220307
LC record available at https://lccn.loc.gov/2022002223
LC ebook record available at https://lccn.loc.gov/2022002224
10 9 8 7 6 5 4 3 2 1

Published by Paraclete Press
Brewster, Massachusetts
www.paracletepress.com

Printed in the United States of America

CONTENTS

INTRODUCTION

L eadership seminars are offered everywhere
these days. Every company takes care to train
its directors and managers so that they can lead
more effectively. But many leadership seminars are
more about methods than about the requirements
of leadership.

When we look at the *Rule* of St. Benedict of
Nursia for leadership models, we find a different
approach. Benedict is primarily concerned with the
question of how someone who is supposed to lead
needs to be constituted, how such a person needs to
work on himself in order to be able to lead at all.
To Benedict, leading through personality is more
important than anything else. Only then does he
offer specific suggestions on how to lead.

Most leadership seminars are about training
leadership skills: clear goal setting, goal-oriented use
of personnel and resources, quickly understanding
complex connections, and making the right
decision. Benedict, on the other hand, describes
the attitude and character of the person responsible
for organizing the monastery—and never loses
sight of the goal of leadership. But that goal is not
maximizing profits. Instead, the goal is dealing
mindfully with the creation and fellow human
beings. For Benedict, the goal of leadership is that

through cooperative work, the house of God is built: a house in which God's glory shines through; a house in which the brothers (in the following, "brothers" always means all sisters as well, of course) can live together in peace and joy, thus bearing witness to God's healing and loving nearness.

At first glance, this goal seems out of touch with the real world. But upon closer inspection, it seems more current than it ever was. Many companies have realized that it is not enough simply to cut costs and maximize worker productivity. What is crucial is for a company to look beyond the narrow idea of maximizing profits and instead find a meaning in its business.

Aside from the many books and seminars on the topic of leadership, in recent years another topic—business ethics—has come to the fore. Company heads and economic policy makers have increasingly recognized that, without ethical principles, it is impossible to lead a company. Ethical principles do not mean moral appeals or moralistic demands, which often have no connection to the realities of business. Often, what the church says on the topic of business ethics has this kind of moralizing undertone—and is therefore not very helpful.

The Caux Round Table, founded by Frits Philips and Olivier Giscard d'Estaing, explains that moral values are essential to decision-making in business, because:

Neither the law nor market forces are sufficient
to ensure positive and productive—in every
sense of the term—conduct.
(Caux Round Table, available at www.cauxroundtable
.org/principles/)

Benedict's *Rule* does not moralize. It sets up
principles which the abbot (the head of the monastic
community) or the cellarer (the monastery's economic administrator) are supposed to follow in
fulfilling their tasks. It shows how economic
function and economic security for a large number
of people can be combined with respecting the
creation and the human beings around us. This path
is what we call leadership.

I myself was cellarer of Münsterschwarzach
Abbey for over thirty years. With the eye of the
person to whom they were addressed, I will not
discuss all statements the *Rule* gives on the subject of
leadership but will limit myself to the chapter on the
cellarer. It is read three times a year during dinner at
the Münsterschwarzach monastery, and each time is
a confrontation with my conscience, whether I have
actually done justice to Benedict's ideas.

Writing about it now, I know that I fall short of
even my own words and ideas. I know the temptation to let things slip, to refuse to lead. And I
also know the urge within me to make a decision
quickly, skipping over the sometimes arduous paths
of decision-making. Nevertheless, I am daring to
write about leadership according to Benedict's

Rule—not because I am so good at it, but because I want to face up to the challenge that the chapter on the cellarer represents. Benedict's words do not leave me be but keep moving me to attempt the sometimes hard but also often enjoyable work of leadership. The more I concern myself with the specific tasks of the cellarer, the more I realize how in touch with reality Benedict's words are.

As a counterpoint to the chapter on the cellarer, I also want to consider the chapter about the abbot of a monastery, which formulates similar principles. But I do not want to apply these principles only to leadership in monastic, pastoral, or ecclesiastical contexts, but also to the situations of the many companies I have advised.

In my conversations with company managers and bank directors, I have found that the thoughts of the *Rule* are not out of touch but can inspire us to look for new forms of leadership. In my lectures, listeners who have no leadership roles in their work have nevertheless shown me that they can apply these thoughts in their everyday lives. All those of us who interact with other human beings are simultaneously leaders and people who are led. Parents raising their children have leadership roles as well. Any group has some members who are leaders and some members who follow—although the roles can frequently switch, as well. One may lead in financial matters, while another person leads when it comes to organizing a party and decorating its location.

How do we interact with others when we take on a leadership role? How do we deal with others in our family, in our parish, in our political party, at work, or in society at large? How do we lead, and how do we let ourselves be led, how do we react to people in a leadership role? We are responsible for how we let ourselves be led. It is never the responsibility of the leader alone, but always also of the follower and what kind of leadership he is willing to accept. So, this book can offer perspectives not just for people who lead but also for people who are led: How do I deal with my leadership role, and how do I deal with being led? How can I change the leadership style of my superior through my reactions to his leadership?

If we look at the kind of leadership models propagated today, we often find that they assume a mechanical model of a business: a business structured like a machine, with precise planning models, organizational hierarchies, and criteria for measuring success. But such businesses tend to be soulless. And leadership in that context often means slashing as many jobs as possible, reducing management and administrative staff, maximizing worker output, and shifting production to a country where labor is cheaper.

But this kind of leadership model is marked by lack of imagination and lack of soul. Working in those kinds of companies simply is not fun.

Contrast this with companies that relate instead, somehow, to chaos theory: "If control and power are the defining characteristics of mechanical organizations, fun and spontaneity are the characteristics of chaotic organizations." The prototype of this kind of chaotic business is Microsoft. One manager said of his employees: "We are able to keep [these employees] because their jobs are meaningful, not because they need the money" (Secretan, 34).

Benedict has a model that is completely different from these two alternatives. He writes of the house of God that a monastery should be. To him, that does not mean simply that the monks go to church often for prayers. He means that this house of God is built by work.

What is interesting is that a leading consultant in the US today talks about businesses as a Sanctuary. He is not referring to a specific location, but to an attitude—a group of people who mobilize their spiritual resources, ask relevant questions, love, trust, and respect one another, speak a common language:

> A Sanctuary is a holy place, a place where we give reverence to all of the people and things within it. (Secretan, 245)

And such a community is a place of joy, inspiration, and love; it is a place where everyone can freely develop their self; where our soul is addressed and supported. When Benedict speaks of the "house of God," he means a community of brothers and sisters who care about one another, in which everyone can blossom because everyone has an inalienable dignity. That is not out of touch, but actually means effective leadership that can lead to strong profits as well—as we see with some companies in the US. It is interesting to me that the Benedictine leadership model, though it is almost 1,500 years old, is new again, and modern enough to answer important questions of our time.

THE QUALITIES
OF A LEADER

The chapter on the cellarer begins with these words:

> The cellarer of the monastery should be chosen from among the community. To qualify for this choice a candidate should be wise and mature in behavior, sober and not an excessive eater, not proud, nor apt to give offense, nor inclined to cause trouble, not unpunctual, nor wasteful, but living in the fear of God, and able to show the community all the love a father or mother would show to their family. (*Rule*, 31:1f)

Benedict here lists some important traits for a cellarer. Before he even begins writing about the art of leadership, he describes the personality of the leader.

The attitude Benedict demands of the cellarer requires that the cellarer has gone through the school of self-knowledge as it was described by the earliest monks. Anyone who wants to lead others must first be able to lead himself: he needs to be able to deal with his own thoughts and feelings, with his own needs and passions.

The early monk Evagrius Ponticus wrote, in his book *Praktikos*, that a monk should first observe himself, in order to recognize what emotions drive him, what needs rise up in him, and what passions lead him. Then, the monk must probe the basis of these thoughts and feelings: what are they trying to tell him? What fundamental problem is making itself felt in them? What has hurt him? What keeps him from thinking clearly?

The monk's actual task, according to Evagrius, is grappling with these passions, which Evagrius calls the nine *logismoi*. Anyone who wants to take a position of responsibility must first have gone through this shaping and training of the self. Otherwise, he will keep conflating his leadership tasks with his unacknowledged needs. Repressed passions will guide his emotions and prevent him from leading clearly. If a leadership personality knows the instruments of organization and control but is emotionally uncontrolled or unbalanced, he may be able to reduce costs in the short term but will in the long term infect the company with his immaturity, hampering employee motivation. All the unconscious needs and emotions will be projected onto colleagues, creating a kind of "emotional sludge" that keeps the company from running smoothly. Everything that is not consciously examined returns as a shadow, with a destructive effect on the environment.

For example, we only need to read Edzard Reuter's memoirs about his time heading the car manufacturer Daimler-Benz in order to see just how much energy is lost through jealousy, rivalries, repressed aggression, and a lack of emotional balance in leaders. That is why it is right for Benedict to place such importance on the character of the leader.

WISDOM AND EXPERIENCE

The first requirement for the task of economic stewardship is that the cellarer be wise. The Latin word Benedict uses here is *sapiens*, which means insightful and discerning. It comes from the root *sapere*, which means to taste, to discern, to know. Someone who tastes things as they are, who does not merely think about them but comes into contact with them, who grasps them with the senses—that person can become wise. He understands things from the inside.

This kind of wisdom is not the same as intelligence or cleverness (*prudentia*). Wisdom always involves experience. The root of the word "wisdom" is an Old English word meaning "to know." But this is not exterior knowledge. Instead, wisdom has to do with seeing and perceiving. Wisdom is the ability to see things as they are. This is why the cellarer needs not knowledge, but wisdom. He must be in touch, literally, with reality. He must have taste, a feeling for what is right, for the things that are. He must have experience with himself and with other human beings.

MATURITY

The second requirement is mature behavior, or mature mores (*maturis moribus*). The word "mature" comes from a root meaning "ripe"—like a fruit that has ripened and can now be harvested. Only a ripe fruit is tasteful. An unripe fruit is bitter or sour and does not agree with us. The task of a cellarer requires a mature human being—only a ripened human being can be enjoyed by those he leads. He must be ripened by rain and sun and have faced up to life. By being open to rain and sun, to the heat of the day and the darkness of the night, the seed within him is transformed.

Criteria for maturity are inner calm, serenity, being whole, being at one with oneself. Someone who is in contact with their own center does not get unsettled so easily. But an unripe, immature person allows habits and behaviors to creep in that do not do good to the people around him. In the newspaper headlines, we are constantly reading about managers who may earn a great deal of money but have nevertheless remained unripened and immature. Even today, employees are still justified in expecting maturity from their leaders.

Otherwise, they lack the motivation to follow their lead, to receive their instructions and do as they are told.

Benedict also lists several characteristics of a mature person. One is sobriety. The Latin word *sobrius* means not being intoxicated, being sober, not subject to lusts, rational, clear-headed. A sober person is one who sees things as they are, rather than gazing at them through the obscuring fog of inebriation. A sober person does justice to the things around him, can give a level assessment of the facts, and is not torn one way or another by emotions. Many people see things not as they are, but through the lens of their own repressed desires, needs, emotions, fears, and mistrust.

In Benedict's view, a person who does justice to things is a mature and spiritual person. Spirituality is not an escape from reality, but the art of doing reality justice, of seeing it as God created it. That may seem easy. But we always experience things as we see them, and often we do not see things correctly. We make ourselves little illusions of reality. We live in the illusion of being able or allowed to make use of everything for ourselves. We imagine we are the greatest and most important people in the world. And then we think that the world should serve us and our ends.

Anyone who goes through the world like this, drunk on their own illusions, will be unable to really lead. Instead, he is much more likely to bring despair upon those for whom he has taken responsibility. Many bankruptcies make it clear that the responsible leaders were subject to some sort of illusion; they could not see reality soberly.

In his memoirs, Edzard Reuter repeatedly describes how strongly a major company like Daimler-Benz is affected by the tensions and conflicts originating in little jealousies and rivalries of colleagues in management. Everyone has their own pet projects and ideas and fights for them, pretending to fight for the larger good of the company. But in reality, the true battleground is one's own power, vanity, and admiration.

If a leader is not mature and does not soberly work for the greater good, then he is simply using his energy to prevent others from working against him, often by encouraging his colleagues to work against one another.

In that way, leadership will never succeed. Energy does not serve a larger goal but only one's own power. That makes it impossible to create a team. Instead, there is "a group of wild animals without anyone to tame them," as a banker is once said to have described the Daimler-Benz management. In such companies, most of the energy is lost through skirmishes over power and influence. Victory in these skirmishes is then achieved by whatever means are possible: Holding out on essential information or ignoring others and simply following one's own plan. If leaders are not concerned with frank discussion and objective improvement, but rather with personal vanity, then the company, and in the long run society, bears the cost. Thousands of jobs are endangered, and everyone is worried about making sure they get one of the best seats—and not with creating an environment that might shape society for the better.

The German philosopher Otfried Höffe, in his book *Moral als Preis der Moderne* (Morality as the Price of Modernity), developed an ecological world ethics with building blocks that correspond to Benedict's two values of wisdom and sobriety (clear-headedness). To him, the two most important ecological virtues are equanimity and thoughtfulness, seen respectively as counterweights to the hubris of scientific positivism and the excesses of technological and economic rationalization (Küng, 248).

The sober attitude that Benedict demands of the cellarer looks at things as they are and places them in appropriate perspective. Today, economic logic does fall easily into excesses. We want limitless growth, ever more money. Only a wise and sober leader will be able to resist this temptation for excess and be satisfied with the scope appropriate to their company.

CONTENTEDNESS

The cellarer should not be "an excessive eater." The Latin word *edax* that Benedict uses does indeed mean gluttonous or excessive eating habits—but it is generally used about animals. A mature human being, on the other hand, is mature because he is able to deal with things in a human way. Often enough, mealtimes do bring out the animal in us. We simply stuff food into ourselves. Someone who truly savors each dish will never eat too much. They will find joy in the culture of the meal, will taste God's gifts in the dishes. Someone who bolts their food, on the other hand, is not in touch with what they are eating.

Psychologists tell us that how we eat tells us a great deal about our relationship with the world. A person who is ravenous toward their food will also behave ravenously toward others, will see others as things to consume and exploit, and will therefore also exploit all of creation. Such a person will see everything around them as something to be used for their own gain. They will be just as eager for money and will seek to constantly increase their possessions and power. Such a person will use anything and everything to increase their success—rather than to serve humanity through their leadership. They will not be concerned with the general welfare, but with their own immeasurable need. And since they can stuff themselves with all kinds of things and never be sated, they will never be satisfied, either. That inner dissatisfaction will infect their coworkers and employees. The result is blindness for the actual tasks of leadership and for a leader's responsibility in society.

What Benedict recognizes as the dangers of "excessive eating" we can today see in many different areas. Top managers, for example, demand expensive hotel rooms, measure their own value in the cost of their travel expenses, their hunting trips, cocktail receptions, or limousine size. Edzard Reuter, who himself traveled a great deal in the course of his work for Daimler-Benz, poses the following question with regard to his colleagues:

> Is it really worthwhile to ponder the addictive allure that travel and accommodation in luxury hotels seem to have for some people? Or how much they can function as stimulants, with all the resulting dangers and feelings of desire? (Reuter, 196)

Unless a person lives out a different value system, they will succumb to this danger again and again. For Reuter, an important antidote was experiences of nature that reminded him "how unimportant you are in the face of the miracle of this earth, [and] ... that your life, too, is finite" (Reuter, 196).

Only those who, like Benedict, look beyond themselves and search for God, rather than their own satisfaction, in all things, will be able to embody the attitudes that the *Rule* demands of the cellarer. A person who orbits themselves will use everything only for their own gain. Having a transcendental reference point puts our addiction to success and possessions in proper perspective. It shows us that life, in the end, is about God, not about success and accomplishments, or profit and income.

HUMILITY

We might refer to the leadership qualities Benedict expects as virtues. That word originally comes from the Latin *virtutes*, meaning "strengths." Only the person who has the strength to internalize virtuous qualities is suitable for leadership. One such quality is humility: Benedict expects the cellarer not to be proud (*non elatus*). A person who is *elatus* holds himself above others, thinks he is better than others. Such a person needs to make others small in order to believe in his own greatness.

Many people abuse their power by making others small and putting them down in order to increase their feeling of self-worth. Benedict requires the cellarer to be humble enough, courageous enough, to look closely at his own humanity. He also says of the abbot that he should always be mindful of his own frailty (*Rule*, 64:13). Humility means accepting one's own frailness and inconstancy; recognizing that one is a person who may constantly misstep or fall, whose life's structure can come crashing down all too easily. Humility is the courage to dive down into one's own humanity, one's own shadow. Instead of rising high, a humble person will get off their high horse and recognize that they are taken from the soil, the earth. (The Latin word for humility, *humilitas*, comes from the word *humus*, meaning "earth.") Only if we accept that part of our nature will we stop setting ourselves over others, and instead deal humanely with them and respect their dignity.

A leader with humility will not arrogantly stride through his company and "turn his nose up" at his employees. Instead, he will empathize with them and reach out to them where they stand. He will understand them—meaning also that he will stand behind them, or stand protectively in front of them, or stand beside them when they have problems.

The psychologist John R. O'Neill sees arrogance and high-handedness as one the greatest dangers for those who have responsibility for companies. He cites the example of a successful Wall Street trader whose financial success led him to bury his spiritual feelings until "more of him was hidden than visible" (O'Neill, 108).

He therefore sees it as leaders' most important task to avoid hubris. He gives us something like a checklist of early warning signs for hubris:

- ✥ Starting to believe we have special powers, including being infallible or immune to human error

- ✥ Seeing people who do not share our views as saboteurs, stupid, jealous, or incapable of contextual thinking

- ✥ Becoming less accessible as leaders, trusting an ever-smaller circle of advisers, or "killing the messenger"

- ✥ Paying too much attention to minor points like correct forms of address, seating arrangements, or the location of the meetings. (List derived from O'Neill, 109ff)

Hubris leads us to stop learning. Our ego keeps inflating, and we believe we can do whatever we want. In reality, we are being led by our repressed shadow, and the more we repress it, the more destructive it becomes. The humility that Benedict demands of the cellarer involves willingness to look closely at the shadow. The integration of what we see, to "meet and eat the shadow," in O'Neill's words, is what ultimately decides whether or not we will have long-term success:

If we continue to stuff such pieces of ourselves into the darkness, we will inevitably pay with the coin of our soul. On the other hand, people who know how to mine their shadow's rich potential and use it for future successes are success sustainers. . . . They [know] how to fight hubris. (O'Neill, 108)

JUSTICE

Benedict then requires the cellarer not to be "apt to give offense"—not coarse or unjust (*non iniuriosus*). *Iniuria* is not simply injustice, however; it is also injury, violence, dishonor, shaming, damage, hurt. A person who leads others must not hurt them.

It is an important psychological rule that a person who does not examine their own injuries is condemned to injure either others or themselves. Or to subconsciously seek out situations in which the injuries of childhood are reenacted, for example. Each of us is hurt throughout our lives. Those injuries are also opportunities for us to grow and to become sensitive to others. But if we do not face up to our own wounds, we will constantly hurt others' feelings—or hurt ourselves. In order to have responsibility for others, Benedict writes, a person must have confronted their own injuries. Taking stock of one's own life story is therefore a prerequisite for leading others well. Otherwise, one's own unexamined life story will become tangled up with one's actual leadership tasks.

Many people believe that leading consists primarily of exerting power. And not a few exercise their power by injuring others or hurting their feelings. When a manager or director has hurt an employee or colleague to the point where they begin to cry or be silent, that may be the only way for that manager to feel his power—but it is not real power. Instead, it is the passing on of one's own pain. If I hurt someone else, I do not awaken life in them, but hinder it.

For this reason, leadership through hurt or force, even violence, is the exact opposite of effective leadership. And yet it happens often that those with leadership responsibilities hurt those who work with them. It can happen while walking through the office in the morning: Instead of looking at each person and greeting them, some see only the mistakes or inadequacies they imagine in their colleagues.

Or there are many small pinpricks of hurt. Especially between men and women, there are many small hurts in companies every day. One example might be a boss who feels the need to constantly put down his secretary in order to show her who is in charge. Deep, personal injuries can occur if I criticize someone's body. If that boss tells his secretary that she is too fat or unattractive, that can cause a deep sense of hurt, in part because she cannot possibly defend herself. There are so many injuries and hurts that occur in our companies because injured or hurt people take on leadership roles and simply pass on their own hurt. But hurt and injuries make us emotionally sick, and they drive up the numbers of people who go off work sick. That more than undoes any gains managers want to achieve through organization and control.

"Non-injurious," or not apt to give offense, is one meaning of the words *non iniuriosus*. The other is simply just: The cellarer should be a just person and do justice to all colleagues and their needs, should treat everyone justly. Justice presupposes that every person has rights that must be preserved, such as the right to be him or herself, the right to freedom, to dignity, to honor and respect.

A leader can only be just if he puts aside his own prejudices. He must first of all look at how many prejudices he still has. Only once he recognizes them can he distance himself from them. The "incorruptibility of judgment" is the paramount requirement for just treatment of individuals, because in order to do right, we must first find a just way of thinking.

Only when I have freed my thinking of its fogginess will I be able to see the human beings around me justly, and only then can I treat them justly. Justice means treating all of them equally, without preferring one over another, without committing any kind of "nepotism." That can lead only to divisiveness and jealousy. Any employee values a boss who is just—even if he is strict! But

if he is just and incorruptible in his judgments, he
will be respected by all.

CALM

The cellarer's next characteristic is that he should
not be "inclined to cause trouble." The original Latin
word is *turbulentus*, meaning unquiet, stormy, full
of confusion, confusing. It comes from the noun
turba, indicating noise, disorder, confusion, disarray,
or a phantom.

A person who is *turbulentus*, troublesome, is
a person who cannot find calm because they are
constantly being controlled by the noise of their
own thoughts, being buffeted by the many different
emotions inside them. Such a person cannot think
clearly; on the contrary, they suffer from great inner
confusion. There are so many emotions clamoring
within them, and they are torn between the different
emotions. Their self becomes like an occupied
house: they are no longer in control but at the mercy
of the "occupiers," their emotions and passions.
Such a person cannot give good leadership. They
will instead cause more restlessness. Their emotions
will enter into anything and everything. And so, an
"emotional sludge" will start to build up around
them.

In some companies, one can feel a swamp of
emotions around a manager, making it more difficult
for all employees to work in a straightforward way.

Even just wading through the swamp takes all the energy one has.

Some people confuse the noise of their thoughts with hecticness and haste, which they spread around them and demand from their employees. But if a manager is constantly heckling his employees for haste, he does not lead them forward. He is simply creating a turbulence that, in the end, moves nothing. If he forces his employees into haste, then in the end he is committing violence, which is the meaning of the root of the word "haste." Because a person who is torn inside hates himself, he will also hate others. Instead of leading them, he will hasten them, drive them into turbulence and confusion. He will cause trouble. He thinks that by spreading the turbulence inside him, he is spurring people on to work. But in such a turbulent, troubled atmosphere it is impossible to work effectively. One has the impression that some managers confuse haste with leadership, that they want to prove themselves by the hectic pace they impose upon themselves and others. But this is not leadership. It is a form of violence against others. It is destructive, not constructive.

Benedict, on the other hand, demands an inner calm from the cellarer. Only someone who is at one with themselves, at peace with themselves and God, will be able to create an atmosphere of calm in which employees can feel comfortable and can enjoy focusing on their work. Strength is never in rushing through something hectically, but in remaining calm. But a leader can only find their own inner calm by not avoiding their own inner truth. That requires being able to face all the things that arise in us in the quiet hours—facing them because we know ourselves loved and accepted fully by God.

DECISIVENESS

The next quality Benedict expects in a cellarer seems all too external: He should be on time, not unpunctual or slow (*non tardus*). Today, discovering the virtue of slowness is a counterweight to the hustle and bustle and ever-increasing pressure of the workplace. But Benedict is certainly not saying that the cellarer should not work conscientiously and with full attention to what he is doing. The meaning of slow is closer to dull of spirit, hesitant, foolish, or stupid.

There is a kind of slowness that suggests that the soul is blocked: Some people are slow because their soul is weighed down by problems. They are too concerned with themselves, so nothing flows. It is as if they are driving with the hand brake on, using too much energy for themselves and their own emotional stability. They have no energy left that might flow outward. The early monks considered effective, skillfully accomplished work the sign of a spiritual person. When someone is in touch with their inner well-spring, with the source of the Holy

Spirit within them, then work will flow out of them. They will send something out into the world.

The Latin word *tardus* also suggests something hesitant. There are indeed people who cannot decide because they are perfectionists.

They are afraid of making mistakes, so they prefer not to make choices. They draw out everything until it is too late to make a decision. On a visit to East Germany, Mikhail Gorbachev is supposed to have uttered the famous words "Those who are late will be punished by life itself." Many people are late because they are afraid to change things, because they fear the consequences of their decision. A person who wants to lead others, however, must decide clearly and quickly. He cannot wait for everything to become completely clear.

To Benedict, a clear choice is a spiritual virtue. It comes from our inner feelings, where a monk listens to the voice of the Holy Spirit within him, trusting that voice. Our inability to decide is often associated with a perfectionist attitude. Because we want to avoid mistakes at all costs, we do not trust ourselves to make decisions. We wait for others to choose for us. But by drawing out the decision, we often do everything wrong.

There are some companies where one feels that the leaders are primarily interested in keeping their jobs. Their most important task, then, is not drawing attention to themselves and not making mistakes. But this means that nothing new can grow: Imagination and innovation are lost. Fearing decisions, one circles around one's own ideas and blamelessness. One cannot look to colleagues and the company, but always egotistically reduces everything to possible consequences for oneself. Consequences for the company become secondary.

Indecision is probably the greatest barrier to true leadership. Employees become dissatisfied in a company that is constantly delaying important decisions and hampering their enthusiasm. They no longer know what to rely on, they wait pointlessly for decisions that never come. While they wait, aggression against company leaders or against one another or themselves can grow. That aggression can then no longer be directed appropriately. It becomes self-destructive, damaging the working environment and keeping the entire company from moving forward.

THRIFT

The cellarer should also be "not wasteful" (*non prodigus*). He should deal carefully with things and not toss them away. The word "wasteful" comes from root words meaning to destroy or despoil. Instead of despoiling wealth, instead of exploiting the creation, the cellarer should show care to all the things that are entrusted to him. He has not been given power over things, but only the task of caring stewardship for the things that are, in order that everything be treated properly, in order that it can serve the purpose it has been given by God.

The need for wastefulness points to a character disturbed by lack of self-worth or by inner chaos. Because a person feels himself to be worthless, he must deal wastefully with things, must show everyone one how much he has. Because he is without internal structure, there is no structure to how he handles the world around him. This action shows the same general structure as in indecisiveness: One uses things for one's own ends, rather than serving the things to their ends. One wastes wealth in order to compensate for one's own feeling of worthlessness with extravagance. Everything is used to serve oneself.

Leading, on the other hand, means serving people and things, having first the good of the people and the company in mind, and not primarily one's own prestige. Dealing well with things requires inner distance from oneself. Freedom from myself, freedom from constantly orbiting my own self. Freedom from the question of what I get out of it.

FEAR OF GOD

Benedict contrasts all the previous "negative" characteristics of what a cellarer should not be with one summarizing, central term—a term we might not expect from a person meant to keep the accounts in order. The cellarer is supposed to be God-fearing (*timens Deum*). Fear of God means being affected by God in the positive sense: I let myself be struck by God, let myself be touched by the things God has given to me. I honor them with mindfulness.

Saint Hildegard of Bingen knew fear of God as a woman whose entire body consists of eyes. This is a watchful, mindful woman, attending to all the things around her with her entire body; a woman who sees God in all things and in all things lets herself be touched and stricken by God.

A God-fearing person has a sense that with his entire existence, he stands before God and is oriented toward God. By demanding that an economic manager fear God, Benedict shows that he sees spirituality not as something purely supernatural, but that it is expressed in careful husbandry as well, in dealing appropriately with things. A person who does not fear God will not handle economic matters carefully, either. This is why economic problems in monasteries always indicate in part that the spirituality of the monastery is not strong enough to include all monastic aspects. The monastery's spirituality may be only liturgical or aesthetic, but it does not have the power to permeate the world. It does not have enough care for the economic situations and financial matters. It ignores economic necessities that must be confronted. It hides behind ideologies in order to avoid facing up to reality. One such ideology is that one should do all the work oneself—that the monastery should not employ outsiders. This shows the monastery is out of touch with reality. It ideologizes work, rather than organizing it properly.

But this happens in businesses just as often as in monasteries. Work is seen as a means to a financial end, and any work that does not turn a spectacular profit is seen as valueless. This ideology is shared between businesses and some monasteries, but in both cases, it loses sight of reality. One has lost that fear of God which means mindfulness and care. Fear of God always also means respect for human beings. It is expressed in regard for human life. To Benedict, fear of God and faith in Christ as revealed in our brothers and sisters are inextricably linked. A person who fears God will also see God's image in humankind.

To many people, the term "fear of God" may sound strange. But fearing God does not mean fearing for oneself. It means a life oriented toward God, rather than oriented toward oneself. Fear of God frees us from human fears. A person who is afraid of making mistakes or of looking foolish in front of others is incapable of leadership. Because however much he may try to lead, he is positioned with respect to himself. He sees others through the lens of what he can "get out of them."

The fear of God frees me from my pathological self-referentiality, from my fear for myself and my success. A person who fears God will gain freedom from the fear of failure, of mistakes, of criticism.

Fear of God liberates me from myself, so that I can see people and things with respect to God, and thus do them justice. I can deal with people and things as is appropriate before God, who made all people and things.

FATHERLINESS

The instruction that a cellarer should be like a father seems far removed from today's world. We rebel against a patriarchal style of leadership. We are aiming for something more collegial, more communicative. But Benedict means something else entirely when he invokes a father (or mother), something that is just as meaningful today. The cellarer should have the qualities of fatherliness both for the community at large and for each individual member. As a child grows up, the father is the one who strengthens its backbone, who gives the child courage to dare things and risk taking one's life into one's own hands.

When a person is missing this experience of fatherliness, when they have never had a father who had their back, this person may often search for some substitute for that stability. Often, they find such a substitute in ideology, in rigid norms, in dogmatic principles.

If, as happens in some companies, everyone hides behind strong norms, that expresses a lack of experience with fatherly safety. The German psychoanalyst Alexander Mitscherlich has written about a "fatherless society." During and after major wars, many children grew up without a father, because he had either fallen or was held captive as a prisoner of war. Additionally, in Mitscherlich's view, many of today's fathers refuse to fulfill their paternal role, leaving many children to grow up without fathers.

If a cellarer is to be like a father, that can mean that he encourages those around him to dare something, to take a risk, to make mistakes. In many companies, employees and leaders alike are afraid of making mistakes. They are thinking of their own position, not about the well-being of the company. If a company is led by managers who do not hold themselves accountable for their actions, who try to find fault with others, who are most anxious about their own careers, then the company will, over the short or the long term, get into difficulties.

In particular, German managers are reputed to have little courage to support their employees in trying something daring. It is clearly hard to give up the old mentality of preferring good followers over risk-takers. But a good father never puts his own prestige above the well-being of the family. He encourages his children, gives them the courage to try new things. He has their back when they start to go their own way. He gives them a credit of trust, so that they can go out and experience the world.

Considering the father as a responsible person, we can develop a different kind of leadership than we see so often today: Not a worried manager focused on their own career, but a leader who awakens life in his colleagues, who strengthens their resolve, gives them courage to go their own way, seek out new solutions. In the same way, Benedict does not want a community that clings, frightened, to old norms. He is looking for a community that has the courage to take risks and walk new paths. The high standards to which Benedict holds potential cellarers demand a hard school of self-knowledge and the willingness to work on oneself. It is impossible to completely change one's character. But if I accept myself as I am, then something within me can be transformed. My negative behaviors can alter.

The more consciously I deal with myself—the more conscientiously and consistently I make an effort to walk my inner path—the stronger will I be able to initiate a process of development. Some managers would do better to take a hard look at themselves and examine their own soul, rather than concern themselves with difficult colleagues or a more efficient organization of the company. Only someone who is self-aware is protected from the falsifying, obscuring influence his unconscious needs and repressed passions can have on true leadership.

HOW TO LEAD—
BENEDICT'S VIEW OF
HUMAN NATURE

Benedict now describes specifically how a cellarer is supposed to fulfill his role—how he is supposed to lead:

> The cellarer will be responsible for the care of all the monastery's goods but must do nothing without the authority of the superior, being content to look after what is committed to the cellarer's care without upsetting other members of the community. If one of the community comes with an unreasonable request, the cellarer should, in refusing what is asked, be careful not to give the impression of personal rejection and so hurt the petitioner's feelings. Such a refusal of an ill-judged request should be given with good reasons and due deference to the person involved. (Rule, 31:3–7)

CARE

The cellarer is responsible for the care of all the monastery's goods. But that he is supposed to care about them does not mean that he should be care-worn. The Latin *cura*, for care, means something more like diligence, as well. He should keep an eye on things, and work thoroughly, if carefully, on the things entrusted to him. He should deal just as caringly with people as with things. Nor does Benedict mean that the cellarer is supposed to do everything on his or her own instead of delegating. A boss who takes care of everything himself, who butts into every tiny matter, is not a role model we would want today.

Nevertheless, we want a manager to have an eye on everything, to organize everything in such a way that those responsible can properly lead and outfit their departments. It is not enough to just look at successes while ignoring how the people are doing. It is not enough to look just at productivity while ignoring the working environment. If I do not pay attention to what kind of work culture and what kind of interactions are shaping the company, the bottom line will start to suffer very soon as well.

Today, Benedict's statement that the cellarer must do nothing without the approval of the abbot seems to indicate submission rather than creativity. But that is not what is meant. The cellarer is supposed to develop his own creativity and introduce new ideas—but he is required to seek the backing of his superior in whatever he does, as well. He cannot simply press through his favorite ideas. He needs to let the abbot, who is above him, double-check them.

Some managers would gain a lot from submitting their ideas to a committee rather than just implementing them as they come along. When a manager is constantly putting his favorite ideas into practice, that creates an undirected restlessness that helps no one in the company. Employees are at the mercy of their superior's whims, and a clear strategy is lost.

The abbot is like a supervisor, double-checking the ideas brought to him by the cellarer. That means that the cellarer must first think through them clearly himself, and that he must be able to formulate them in a way that will convince the abbot. This ensures that, rather than every unripe idea being put into action, a good continuity is maintained.

MINDFULNESS

In Benedict's original Latin, his next instruction for the cellarer is: *Quae iubentur custodiat*—he shall look after what is committed to his care. *Custodire* means to watch over, care for, observe, protect. Benedict's concern is mindfulness: The cellarer should not simply accept each of the abbot's instructions regardless of their content. Instead, he should think about what those instructions mean, and examine the sense behind the abbot's wishes.

It is not primarily a question of obedience, but of mindfulness for the things that are demanded of one. It is about exercising care in all decisions and dealing mindfully and caringly with others.

BELIEVING IN THE GOOD

Benedict's understanding of leadership is revealed in his instruction to the cellarer not to upset or hurt his brothers. Instead, the cellarer is supposed to respect everyone, including those who come to him with unreasonable requests. This reveals Benedict's view of human nature: there is a core of good within each human being, even those who seem apparently unreasonable, who follow only their own wishes. Benedict demands that even they be respected.

Leadership does not mean that I put others down or devalue them. Many people in positions of leadership misuse their power in this way. They make others dependent on their whims: if someone needs something, he must first ask his boss and grovel before him, so that the boss can then prove his own magnanimity. Money is especially easy to abuse to hurt others. If I let someone in need of money feel that he doesn't deserve any, that person will feel hurt.

Benedict calls on me to see Christ in every human being, that I discover the core good in each person. If I believe in Christ in my brother and sister, I will not overlook their mistakes—but I will not reduce them to their mistakes. I will look through their weaknesses and the dark sides of their character and to their good core. But that also allows the other person to believe in the good core within him or herself.

The example of the US energy provider Wisconsin Public Service Corporation (WPSC) shows how important a leadership tool the strategy of never upsetting a colleague by personal rejection can be. WPSC issued company-wide guidelines designed to make sure that its employees were not hurt or personally mistreated in the course of their work, but instead uplifted and encouraged.

These guidelines included:

✤ We cannot tolerate actions that crush people's self-esteem, aspirations, individuality, or dignity;

✤ We must recognize that every employee adds value to the company; therefore, we must not allow job titles to stand in the way of an employee's ability or willingness to contribute; . . .

✤ Work should enrich and bring joy to everyone. (Secretan, 202)

When we encourage our employees and give them the opportunity to do fulfilling, joyful work, the company will flourish in the long run. But if we use our staff to "plug holes," moving them from position to position in order to simply keep the most important posts manned, they will feel deadened and sad in their work.

Leadership, in contrast, means motivating people, encouraging their creativity, giving them wings to fly. "Plugging holes" is not leadership. We must not look only at the posts we need to fill and then distribute them to the personnel we already have available. This kind of thinking, sadly, is far too common in monasteries. Women with good theological education and great artistic skill, for example, are put in the kitchen because that is where someone is needed at the time.

Leadership as envisioned by Benedict means first looking at the people who are around us, and supporting them. We must organize the tasks according to the people, not the other way around. But that does also require our colleagues to be flexible—because an individual person is never called to one post alone but has the potential to work effectively and meaningfully in many different places.

Faith in a person's good core does not require a manager to simply fulfill every wish put before him. He is allowed to say no, and to correct wishes where appropriate. But only ever in such a way that the other person does not feel like a loser or put down or unvalued. Anyone who leads others will be confronted with some number of irrational wishes and demands (*inrationabiliter postulat*). He should not overlook these but find the courage to address the things that are negative and irrational. But even difficult, critical conversations with a colleague should never be about hurting a person or making them feel personally rejected. That leads only to a loss of motivation. The goal of such a conversation is always to build up that person's motivation, which can succeed only if I criticize not the person, but their behavior.

Addressing negative behavior in a non-hurtful way is most likely always a fundamental problem of leadership. Management trainer Fritz J. Schürmeyer, in a seminar for leaders at our monastery, gave us similar guidelines for conversations with colleagues as Benedict himself urges. Schürmeyer's most important rule:

> Offer your colleague the truth as a cloak which he can put on, not as a wet towel you snap around his ears. (Schürmeyer, 2)

In order to talk with a colleague about problems they are causing, we must respect that colleague as a person. We need good will, so that we can look together for ways to contribute both to our colleague's well-being and that of the company. We need serenity, in order to be able to assess and agree to decisions that turn out differently than we had thought. And we need to bring plenty of understanding to the table, even if our colleague is unwilling to understand us (cf. Schürmeyer, 7).

Benedict writes that the cellarer should refuse an unreasonable request (*male petenti deneget*). *Denegare* means to say no to something, to reject it, or to deny it. A person wanting to fulfill every wish is often afraid of rejection—in the end, becoming dependent on those by whom he wants to be loved. Benedict presupposes that a cellarer can also say no, that he must be able to address whatever is unreasonable or negative (*male* means bad, evil, wrong). But he must never do so because of his own mood, and he must always remember the dignity of the individual. He must do justice to the person in front of him, rather than identifying them with their over-reaching requests.

Whenever the cellarer says no, it must not be done emotionally, but *rationabiliter*, meaning sensibly or rationally. He must give his reasons for saying no. The petitioner should understand why his request is being denied, so that he can feel he has been taken seriously.

The leader must remain "reasonable and thoughtful throughout the discussion, even if the other party reacts emotionally" (Schürmeyer, 7). He is responsible, in other words, for ensuring that the conversation does not end in mutual accusations but in reasonable discourse. This requires inner clarity and fortitude—and a healthy distance, so that I do not let myself get carried away by the other's or my emotional reactions.

The Latin word *ratio* means not only "reason," but also "calculation." In his rejections, that is, the cellarer should be "calculable." The petitioner must be able to figure out for himself what requests will likely be successful or unsuccessful. Calculation requires justice. Rejection should not originate in chance or a mood, but in clear reasons, articulated in a transparent logic.

POSITIVITY

In Benedict's view, it is important for a leader to communicate and instigate tranquility and peace, joy and happiness with life. In this, Benedict is in the tradition of the Desert Fathers, a loose group of early Christian ascetics. One of these Desert Fathers is said to have told one of his young students:

Do not make your brother dejected, for you are a monk.

Here, a monk is being actually defined as someone who will not sadden others. The Latin word *contristet* in Benedict's text means to sadden, dishearten, hurt, or harm someone. By insulting someone or hurting their feelings, I am causing sadness and dejection in them. That sadness and dejection will literally dishearten them, robbing them of the heart to keep going.

The subject of sadness was on the mind of many of these ancient monks: evidently, quite a number of them had to do battle with the "demon of sadness." Saint Basil the Great distinguished between God-given sadness, which can lead us to contemplation and salvation, and worldly sadness, which leads to death. This kind of sadness paralyzes. In chapter ten of *Praktikos*, Evagrius Ponticus held that it occurs as the result of frustrated desires or as a result of anger.

The cellarer often has to deny the wishes of the monks. He cannot fulfill every wish—but he must never frustrate their desires for attention and earnest consideration. If these deeply human desires are not fulfilled, the brother will go away saddened and filled with a sense of self-pity and meaninglessness. Such feelings paralyze the brother's work. Conversely, respecting an individual's dignity improves their work performance.

A leader will always hurt the feelings of his colleagues if he himself feels hurt by something. He will pass on his own hurt and sadness. So, he must always confront his own feelings of hurt and make peace with them. Only in this way will he become free from the need to put down or sadden others. This process allows him to see through the old patterns of his life, the patterns that make it harder for him to perceive the needs of his co-workers. Once he can see clearly, he will no longer be as prone to sadden those around him.

Every boss is responsible for their own mood. Some spread a feeling of sadness around them—even if this is not immediately apparent. The manager may seem friendly, even cheerful on the outside and be able to entertain an entire department with his jokes. But that facade masks a deeper sadness, and this sadness slowly settles on his co-workers and creates a depressing work environment.

The solution is not simply for the leader to change his behavior and appear more friendly to his colleagues. He must also face up to his unconscious aspects—his shadow—and consciously engage with them so that they do not have a destructive effect on the workplace. All of us are responsible for the disposition we project.

But I cannot change my disposition overnight. There is no trick that will give a person a positive outlook and allow them to project positivity. Instead, the feeling we project is a result of intellectual honesty with oneself. Honestly facing up to one's own shadow side is often painful and humiliating. Many of us, including those in leadership positions, shirk this hard work. But if we do, the repressed emotions and thoughts are transferred to our co-workers and depress the mood. It is never good for a community when there are winners and losers. That is why a leader should never give those under him the feeling that they cannot change his mind and always have to bow to his will. No one wants to be the permanent loser. Either they will throw in the towel completely and put in only the minimum of effort, or they will plan their revenge.

Since a co-worker can almost never openly best the boss, they will seek victory in inner retreat or refusal: ignoring or sabotaging their superior's instructions. Such employees will obey the letter of the law while permanently irritating their boss and trying to make him feel powerless. The boss can criticize them as often as he likes, and outwardly, the coworkers will always promise to fulfill all tasks to everyone's satisfaction. The urge to refuse will grow so strong in their subconscious that it will eventually also assert itself in the outward reality.

This unconscious resistance often takes the form of simply forgetting the task or letting it wait. Forcing their superior to wait is a hidden way of letting him feel their aggression. This makes it a favorite power game for "small-time bureaucrats." Wherever a bureaucrat has power, he will let others wait, for example if the accounting department flexes its muscles by denying other departments necessary information or making them wait longer than they might need to.

There are many such power plays that the "losers" use to perpetrate revenge on the apparent "winners" of company politics. These power games can paralyze or even tear apart the entire structure of an organization. Since this resistance through power games, forgetting, or wait times comes from the unconscious, the leader cannot overcome it effectively, and those who feel they have "lost" can feel the triumph of "winning": Their boss feels powerless, and his attempts to improve matters with criticism or control are doomed to failure. The number of those who feel an urge to resist are too great, and will continue to grow, eventually infecting and paralyzing the entire company.

The fundamental rule that the cellarer must never hurt the brothers' feelings could have a healing effect in today's business world, as well. Today, we have long since recognized that emotional hurt has a negative effect on bodily health, and that it is therefore possible to get a sense of the workplace environment by how many people are sick or call in sick. When employees feel that they are not being taken seriously, they are more likely to get sick. When they are hurt and put down, these emotional injuries get expressed physically, as well.

A person who spreads fear throughout the firm, therefore, may increase work performance in the short term, but over the long term creates a demotivating, literally sickening climate which reduces performance. The environment is poisoned—and soon, employees too are trying to pass on to their colleagues the hurt they have received.

> The toxification of the office results in anger, resentment, betrayal, and people whose fuses are so short that they resort to snarling at each other. . . . In the toxic organization, the soul is trashed. (Secretan, 74)

If a manager keeps putting down and hurting those who work for him, it is not surprising that "hazing" soon creeps into the company. A person who feels wounded wounds others. A fearful person will pass that fear down the hierarchy. A powerless person will try to compensate for his powerlessness by exerting power over others and bullying them out of the company.

In the year 1995, the car maker GM spent more on healthcare for its employees than it did on steel purchases. These healthcare costs raised the price of each car by approximately $900. These are the results of a business strategy that values victory over competitors higher than the emotional and physical health of its employees.

RESPECT

The cellarer must show respect to his brothers. He must not disdain them (Benedict's Latin *spernere* means to disdain, reject, dislike, show personal antipathy). Showing disdain for another person is an act of casting them out from the community. It casts them into solitude.

Often, my disdain for others is an expression of my inability to accept aspects of myself—and therefore of my disrespect for myself. But because I cannot face up to these emotions, I can express the disdain which I actually have for myself by turning it against others, often those who are weaker in some way.

Disdain saddens and paralyzes; it cuts off relationships among one another and causes a lack of motivation. Instead of disdaining or disrespecting them, a manager should love his employees, accept them in their individuality, encourage and uplift them. This creates not only a healthier workplace environment, but a more productive one, too.

In recent years, many companies have treated the customer as king: each customer or client must be treated with friendliness. This is surely a good thing. But if the company's employees do not feel that they are being treated with friendliness by management, then the strategy of outward friendliness functions like a boomerang for company staff: They are constantly being asked to treat others with understanding and respect while receiving none themselves. Eventually, they will begin either to express their frustration and dissatisfaction outwardly or to internalize them to such a degree that they become emotionally and physically unhealthy. They will soon hate their work and begin to look for work elsewhere.

A company must therefore first of all ensure that its employees' emotional needs are met. The hotel chain Marriott loses up to sixty percent of its service staff annually, simply because they demand too much of their employees. But finding a replacement for a worker who has left costs $1000, so that it is easy to see that a standard mechanical strategy, "where people are viewed as nothing more than parts or production units, rather than souls," not only harms employees, but also negatively affects customer service and the company's bottom line (Secretan, 83).

Hal Rosenbluth, who built one of America's most successful travel agencies, suggests:

> It's our people who provide service to our clients. The highest achievable level of service comes from the heart. So, the company that reaches its people's hearts will provide the very best service. (Secretan, 84)

LEADERSHIP AS SERVICE

Benedict's chapter on the tasks of the cellarer is not entirely systematic. After the brief description of how the cellarer is to carry out his duties, Benedict continues:

> The cellarer's own spiritual progress should be a matter of concern in line with St. Paul's saying that those who give good service to others earn for themselves a good reputation. The cellarer should show special concern and practical care for the sick and the young, for guests and for the poor, and never forget the account to be rendered for all these responsibilities on the day of judgment. (*Rule*, 31:8f)

CONCERN FOR ONE'S SOUL

Benedict's command that the cellarer should have concern (*custodiat*) for his own soul and spiritual progress runs alongside the command to heed what the abbot tells him. The Latin verb *custodire* means to attend to, to guard, to observe consciously. In other words, the cellarer should be in touch with his soul. He should not pay attention only to the commands of others and to external things, but to his soul above all.

Soul refers to our interior space. The soul is where we hear the quiet voices that tell us what is right for us. In the soul, we are in touch with God and our true self. Concern for the soul, therefore, means that in our position as leaders we must not become so involved with external decisions and actions that we lose touch with ourselves. For that, we need silence, in order to be able to hear the quiet voices within us. Daily meditation is therefore not a luxury for the cellarer, but practically a requirement for being able to fulfill his duty well. The cellarer should be centered in himself, and that should be reflected in his actions. In order to really enter into dialogue and relationship with other people and things he first must be in contact with himself, with the things that are going on inside him. And that relationship with himself, with his soul, is simultaneously a relationship with God.

The consultant cited above, Lance Secretan, speaks of "soul-management." With this, he means a leadership style that incorporates aspects of the soul at all levels of decision-making. A person who attends to his own soul can also inspire the souls of his coworkers. He can engage with their deepest longings and can thus motivate them to do good work better than if he just offered them a pay raise. Concern for one's own soul is not outdated. On the contrary, it is the prerequisite for leadership that rewards people not merely financially, but spiritually as well:

We long for leaders who will regenerate our
organizations and create the appropriate
environment in which our souls can flourish.
(Secretan, 27)

But having concern for one's own soul and
spiritual progress also means caring for one's own
soul, for oneself. The cellarer, throughout his work,
must never forget himself, his own needs and wishes,
his passions and emotions. He must be able to feel
how he is being changed by his work: whether what
he is doing is in harmony with his soul, with those
quiet impulses we hear within us. Unconscious
action is always dangerous. A person who is out of
touch with his own needs will inevitably project
them onto others. The things in our actions that
remain unconscious will have a disastrous effect on
the people around us.

Often, we cannot say why a person appears so
unpleasant to others. Often, they are projecting
precisely that which they have repressed. But a
person who is in contact with themselves—who
shows concern for their own soul—will quickly find
contact with others, as well. But a person with no
care for themselves, led only by external tasks and
duties, will not realize how all the repressed needs
fall back upon them. They will work themselves to
the bone without realizing that they are becoming
ever more aggressive and sensitive. Only a person
who has concern and care for their own well-being

will be able to care for the well-being of others and see what others and the community at large need. Otherwise, such a person will soon be burnt out and spread their distemper to their co-workers through sarcastic and cynical comments.

That is why I am always skeptical when a person sets up overly high goals for their task, such as saying they would go all out for the company, or (in a monastery) would fulfill the cellarer's duties out of pure obedience to the abbot. When someone gives themselves up for an organization but loses out themselves, they will become bitter, and their colleagues will sense this bitterness. I myself did not choose the role of cellarer. I fulfilled it out of obedience. But I also know that I would not have been a good cellarer out of pure obedience, if I had had to give up my innermost convictions. I am always responsible for myself, to see that I am fulfilled by the duties.

Of course, this does not mean that I make my enjoyment the highest priority, nor that I do only the things that are fun for me. Any position of responsibility will bring its share of problems. But if I confront these problems and solve them, it does me personally good, as well. If I agree to do a job, I must ensure that it is well with my soul, too. I am responsible for fulfilling my task in a way that is appropriate to me and brings my soul satisfaction.

THE SPIRITUAL PATH OF LEADERSHIP

Benedict then cites a passage from the First Epistle to Timothy:

Those who serve well as deacons gain a good standing for themselves and great boldness in the faith that is in Christ Jesus. (1 Timothy 3:13)

These words are addressed to the deacons. The good standing that a deacon gains if they serve their community well refers in part to the deacon's position in the congregation. But it can also refer to inner standing, a kind of degree of maturity or degree of spiritual insight. Gnostic scholars have used the word *bathnos* (degree or standing) in this way. But Benedict cites only the first part of the verse. He clearly means that those who serve as leaders and serve well will experience inner growth and also grow closer to God. True leadership, then, is a spiritual path, not just pure method. And along this path, we can approach God as surely as we can through prayer.

I feel that in today's world, it is more important than ever to return our focus to the spiritual dimension of leadership. Many managers have begun to realize not only that they must walk paths of relaxation and meditation in order to improve their leadership, but that leadership in and of itself is a spiritual task. Secretan refers to this spiritual dimension of leadership as "delivery," which he defines as "being respectful to the needs of others and having a passion for meeting them." (Secretan, 46)

This delivery is a kind of devotion, and as such is closely linked to love. In the end, leadership requires that the leader love those he leads, and that he be devoted to ensuring their well-being, their fulfillment in their work, and their ability to grow through their work. Because the Church has long emphasized passive virtues, such as obedience and patience, we have overlooked that leadership itself is a spiritual task. Leading others is just as spiritually challenging as prayer and meditation. I am forced to confront the question of whether I am truly, fully engaging with others and therefore with God; whether I am offering my service to God and am prepared to devote myself to the people around and to the cause—whether I am prepared to "deliver."

This question confronts me so radically with my own emotions and repressed needs that I can no longer escape the truth within me. Since only truth can set us free, my leadership role can set me free from my illusions and my entanglement in my own ego. This drives me further and further toward God as the actual foundation upon which I can build.

SERVING LIFE

Benedict's citation of the First Epistle to Timothy makes it clear that he sees economic leadership as a service. The original Greek word used in the epistle is *diakonein* and actually means waiting at table. Serving someone a meal also means supporting their life: it encourages their enjoyment, enables them to feel joy and therefore true aliveness through the food that is served.

Leadership, more than anything else, means awakening this kind of fullness of life in others, coaxing others into a fulfilled and fulfilling life. Benedict's idea of leadership as a service has its origins in a sentence Jesus spoke at the Last Supper. In answer to an argument among the disciples about which one of them is greatest, Jesus says:

The kings of the Gentiles lord it over them; and those in authority over them are called benefactors. But not so with you; rather the greatest among you must become like the youngest, and the leader like one who serves. (Luke 22:25f)

Jesus here makes clear how he understands leadership and distinguishes it from a widespread misconception. Many kings think that leadership consists in ruling over others, putting others down. In the same way, some managers feel the need to put others down in order to believe in their own status. They abuse their power in order to play themselves up. In the above passage, the Greek word used is *kyrieousin*, to act lordly. In other words, they are high-handedly saying to those beneath them: "I am the master, you are the slave. I am everything, you are nothing. I have power over you, and you must do as I say."

Even today, there are plenty of politicians and business leaders who behave this way toward others because they lack an internal feeling of self-worth. They must make others feel bad in order to feel good about themselves. They let others call them benefactors, use their power to burnish their prestige, their image. Their leadership serves themselves, not others. But to Jesus, leadership means service.

The Greek word for leading is *hegemonai*, to walk ahead, to guide, to go in front of. A person who leads others must walk ahead of them, walking the same path as they do. It is not a matter of commanding from on high, but of blazing the trail for those who follow. A leader does himself what he expects of those who follow him.

A person who leads in this way serves his followers. Jesus uses the same word as is used in the Epistle to Timothy: *diakonein*. A person who truly wants to lead should serve—serve life and awaken life in others. Rather than immediately sanctioning a dissatisfied employee who is irritating his co-workers, for example, it would be far better to put oneself in his shoes and meditate on what he may need deep within him. Why might he be so unhappy? What might he be suffering from or longing for? What would do him good? If I strengthen his longing and his dreams, I am being more supportive of his life than if I react only to his superficial mistakes. Leadership of this kind is active. It coaxes out of each person the potential, the life, that is slumbering within them. It motivates each person to develop the gifts God has given them. Leadership is the art of finding the key that will unlock the treasure of those around us, giving them the feeling that they are filled with potential and capabilities. Leadership means arousing others' joy in the development of their own potential and service to the community.

Many of today's management consultants have rediscovered that leadership and service go hand in hand. The German consultant Dr. Hanns Noppeney cites Hans L. Merkle, the director of the German engineering firm Bosch, who advocated in 1979 that "leading and serving are not opposites, but that suitability for leadership is determined by willingness to serve. This makes leading a particular type of serving" (Noppeney, 15f).

Of course, serving a company and its employees does not mean letting oneself be exploited by them. Instead, one must be prepared to take responsibility and shoulder the blame when there are problems. But the serving leader must also be able to distance himself well in order not to be "eaten up" by his own service and work. This is one reason why Benedict counsels the cellarer to attend to his own soul.

Today, the press expects that, if a company has encountered turbulence, the solution is to hire a man of action who, in record time, will "turn the company around" and refurbish it. But these short-term successes often come at a cost to the people of the company. A leader who serves the people will be a blessing for the company over the long term. In contrast, the restlessness with which typical "men of action" box through laboriously planned development measures in an attempt to prove themselves does not really lead to success. Most of the costly change strategies fail. In fact, according to one statistic, 70 to 80 percent of all change processes in companies either flop or peter out (cf. Noppeney, 2).

Every company must be constantly open to changes, or it will stagnate. But if changes are implemented for their own sake, without any reference to the actual needs of the people who work in the company, or if management is using the overhaul as a way to prove itself, the changes come to nothing.

Any good strategy always serves the people, never a manager's self-image. A typical man of action, in trying to implement his theoretical concept heedless of the people of the company, is not actually leading but using the staff as a canvas for his own self-aggrandizement. Or he is using his strategic concept to prove to the world around him that he is a capable, decisive man of action.

Such egotistical methods of leadership do not serve the people they are meant to lead. They only serve the manager's self-image. The result is resistance from the company's employees, who are secretly clamoring to be "saved from the savior" (cf. Noppeney, 3). Contradicting the Darwinist principle that the strongest survive, Noppeney asks critically whether "the man who is willing to serve might not in the end be the better leader, and in the long term deliver better economic results" (Noppeney, 18).

AWAKENING CREATIVITY

Leadership is a creative task. Its goal is to awaken creativity in employees. Secretan writes that a manager should "nourish the soul" of his co-workers. This is another metaphor for helping a person fulfill their potential. Leading is more than simply reacting to the mistakes people make. It is active, imaginative, requires sensing what wants to fulfill itself in someone else.

One way of awakening life consists in communicating to workers the significance and meaning behind what they are doing. If a person is simply concerned with assembling a technological product that happens to be a pacemaker, they will never be highly motivated. But if they are aware of the contribution they are making to saving people's lives, they will feel every impulse to work carefully and eagerly.

A manager is a person who looks beyond the daily dimensions of work, keeps reminding others of the meaningful nature of their work, and lets others participate in his vision. This awakens new skills, new energy, new imagination, new solutions—often by the employees themselves—to better serve people. To me, creativity is the most central trait a manager must have today.

If a leader is not personally very creative, they can at least ensure that the work environment supports creativity, for example by questioning company structures and giving workers the room to develop innovative strategies. (cf. Noppeney, 20) Creativity is also an important sign of spirituality. For that reason, I see creative leadership, developing imagination, as an expression of leadership's spiritual aspect. And this aspect is exactly what Benedict is concerned with. The cellarer must be in touch with his soul, with the source of the Holy Spirit that wells up within him and from which he can draw new ideas.

To a certain extent, creativity and imagination can be taught—so I consider it important that leaders are willing to keep learning from other leaders again and again. In monasteries, unfortunately, it is particularly the superiors who rarely use opportunities for conferences or seminars. And yet we could never lead a community in the same way we did thirty years ago—not spiritually, not economically, and not interpersonally. We need to continually gather new impulses so that we can do justice to the community and its complex inner workings.

HEALING

Benedict continues by stating that the cellarer should extend his service particularly to those who are sick or poor, as well as to children and guests. Children and guests (*hospites*) here stand in for all those who are defenseless or have no rights. Leadership, in Benedict's view, means healing the sick, helping them to live well with their disease.

A leader who is constantly pointing out to his co-workers how they are neurotic or prey to this or that complex and deficit will discourage and humiliate them. Leading means awakening life in the sick by caring for them, by considering what does them good.

Benedict admonishes the cellarer that, with respect to the sick and the poor, he should *cum omni sollicitudine curam gerat*—that is, care with all solicitude. The word solicitude comes from *sollus*, meaning entire, or whole. Benedict, here, is employing a rhetorical doubling to make it very clear that it is the entire heart that should be devoted to caring for the sick and poor. He should weigh in his heart what a sick or poor person might need to live fully. And this does not mean only those sick in body, for whom the cellarer is to build up a working healthcare operation, or the economically poor, to whom the cellarer should give alms. Instead, Benedict is addressing the question of how a leader deals with his fellows who are sick at heart—how he can support them and contribute to their healing.

In any company, there are people who are sick or weak. In Benedict's view, it is not enough simply to tolerate them, to carry them along as "welfare cases." The cellarer, rather, must devote himself with his whole attention and heart especially to those around him who are sick, so that they too can live a fulfilled life and enjoy working, according to their abilities. In fact, assigning a sick person suitable work is a highly efficient form of therapy. It does not involve analyzing the past, but it shows the sick person a goal they can reach. When the sick person pursues that goal with all the strength they happen to have, their wounds heal better than if one is constantly picking at them through analysis.

RECOGNIZING THE SIGNS OF THE TIMES

In today's context, care for the sick and the poor also means considering the social responsibility of every leadership role. The poor do not live only in third-world countries for which monasteries or NGOs collect donations. Today, the question must also be how companies can contribute to creating jobs for the unemployed in our own communities. Creating these sorts of positions requires creativity.

Creative and imaginative economic leadership will always also help other people participate in its projects. Both imagination and the courage to dare create employment. Simply moving production to another country because labor there is cheap would tend to show a lack of imagination: eventually, wages there will rise as well, and then production needs to be moved again. Today, it seems that the most common strategy for rebuilding a company consists of layoffs. But this creates a vicious circle that has devastating consequences for society.

Instead, the goal must be to make meaningful use of the resources that we have at home, to awaken the potential that is sleeping in every worker, to travel new paths in order to use available skills appropriately and thus increase income. Today's unemployment needs other solutions than those practiced by most companies. Instead of complaining about the economics of today, it would be far more sensible to develop creativity and offer products that can meet the needs of our time.

Many managers attribute unemployment or poor company performance to the recession or the structures of today's labor market. They use these arguments to distract from the fact that they have grown out of touch, incapable of drawing and retaining employees and/or customers. In conversation with these kinds of leaders, consultant Lance Secretan has found that "'Recession' is an excuse invented by the irrelevant." (Secretan, 183)

In every recession, there are some companies that "boom." Evidently, these companies had managers who recognized the signs of the times and discovered what people's needs were in the moment. But there are plenty of managers who ignore the times in which they live:

> Their organizations no longer inspire employ-
> ees and suppliers and excite and delight their
> customers. They make products or provide
> services that are **no longer relevant to their
> customers' needs**. (Secretan, 184, emphasis
> in original)

Every company and organization must keep ask-ing itself whether it is in time with the moment, whether it is doing justice to people's current needs, and whether it is making the best use of the resources its employees offer.

DELEGATING RESPONSIBILITY

I hear many complaints in monasteries about overwork. I rarely have sympathy for those complaining, because in most cases I see that as yet another expression of lack of imagination, here disguised as unwillingness to organize the existing work in a new or different way. Often, the workload and distribution are attributed to an ever-decreasing size of the monastic community, which means that the same amount of work has to be shouldered by fewer people. But on the other hand, contemplative monasteries in particular are often unwilling to give important tasks to hired staff.

To me, the idea that all work must be done by the monks themselves is simply ideology. The monastery has a social responsibility as well. Many people would be overjoyed to find work in a monastery. And some sisters and brothers would be better able to fulfill their potential if they were working in other areas of the monastery than busying themselves in kitchen tasks that do not suit them. Many sisters are "kept small" rather than challenged by receiving true responsibility. When a 45-year-old nun must ask her superior what to do rather than make her own free decisions about how to organize her work, her creativity is stifled, and her motivation will decrease.

If I support others in living their potential, if I nourish their soul instead of drowning them in busy work, the result will be a great long-term gain for the monastery—including financially. Once a sister is allowed to make use of her own true strengths and skills, she will be able to earn the monastery far more money than if she is being inundated with cleaning work.

This is always the manager's responsibility. A manager must have an eye for the strengths of the people in their community, in this case, of their confreres in the monastery. They must be in touch with all aspects of monastery operations, and they must constantly look for alternatives that might improve the economic footing of the monastery. In addition, they must lead their employees and co-workers well, or else they will soon start misusing the monastery as their own personal milk cow.

SOCIAL AND SOCIETAL RESPONSIBILITY

Care for the poor also extends to the question of a just distribution of wealth. Benedict is not advocating some romantic ideal of poverty—in fact, he is not speaking of poverty at all, but of simplicity, frugality, and caring for those who do not have enough. A monastery does not have any heal-all recipes for distributing the world's resources fairly. But because it is involved in today's economy and the goods of this world, it must consider how to respond to the world's economic interactions.

Surely it is not enough to simply take everything at face value. But behaving like a superior, moralistic know-it-all does not help either. Leadership today requires looking past the narrow purview of our own organization. It is not enough to do better than other companies—because whatever hurts our competition will not in the long term be to our advantage, either.

Today's entrepreneurs have a social responsibility for the whole of society, even for the entire world. They cannot bow out of responsibility with the excuse that looking after their own employees is more than enough work. Unfortunately, many companies still think in such combative categories. They develop strategies for pushing other companies out of the market and emerging victorious against their competitors. But if I eliminate my competition, I will soon find myself without customers. Winning at a cost to others does not help me in the long term. The art is to win in such a way that everyone else profits as well. Secretan, who has himself built a company with revenues in the hundreds of millions of dollars, describes the destructive potential of competitive thinking:

> Competition creates personal stress, weakens physical and mental health, causes low self-esteem, demotivates, toxifies organizations, damages personal relationships, and is an ineffective way to build teams. It focuses on the negative energy of destroying an opponent instead of the positive energy of enhancing value for employees, suppliers, or customers by meeting their needs. (Secretan, 139)

He sees the task of an entrepreneur as awakening love in our souls, rather than pursuing hostile emotions that wear down and destroy others. In this way, a company has some responsibility for all of society. The ethical values lived within a company affect the entire society.

Whenever a company thinks in combative categories, it increases the aggressive potential in its environment, contributing to a cold, hostile climate. But when a company cares for its employees as well as for its customers and its suppliers, that care will also have a positive effect on the company's surroundings. Leadership means taking responsibility for these surroundings, for society at large. And only someone who is willing to take on this responsibility for the world as a whole deserves to be entrusted with a leadership role today.

LEADERSHIP AND EDUCATION

Benedict also recommends that the cellarer should care for the young. At the time, children were sent to monasteries in order to be educated there. Instead of subjecting them to the strictness of the *Rule*, monks should take into account that the young are not yet as strong as adults. The cellarer is therefore instructed to care especially for the young; one could say that leadership, to a certain degree, is also a task of education.

There are also many "children" working in our companies—people who have remained stuck in a childish stage of their personal development. Leadership means awakening life in these infantile persons, to enable them to grow with their tasks, to mature and become ready to accept responsibility. There is no point in complaining about the childishness of one's colleagues. How these colleagues behave is partly a question of the leadership they receive. The leader is responsible for making sure employees can grow and develop. They do not need to be able to do everything right away. What is crucial is that I can awaken in them the joy of growth and maturing.

Not only is any leadership role also an educational role, but conversely, any educational work is leadership, as well. Any mother and father, in the end, has a position of leadership. Therefore, what Benedict writes about the cellarer is also true of anyone with children. Education, literally and in the root of its meaning, means leading out. As the Latin word *educare* describes it, an educator leads the child out of irresponsibility and unawareness into the unique and splendid image that God has made for himself of this child. Education is often described as a process of shaping or forming, as well. This metaphor means that a person discovers and recognizes their own deeply personal, unmistakable image of themselves—an image that God has made, their true self—and imagines themselves into this image, shapes themselves into it, makes it their own. An educator's role is to support children and young people in this process of self-shaping and forming—to challenge them so that their growth does not stagnate or take a wrong turn, to coax into bloom the life that God has intended for them.

Benedict calls on the cellarer to care for the young with all diligence, to deal with them caringly, to attend to what they truly need and what does them good. Only that allows the young to grow into the shape that corresponds to their innermost image. There is a beautiful text from one of St. Anselm's early biographies, penned by his student Edmar. In the story, St. Anselm admonishes an abbot that he should not limit children with threats or corporal punishment, but should surround them with love, kindness, goodwill, and gentleness—or else he would be sowing the seeds in them of hate and ill will. He offers the image of an artist making a beautiful figure of gold:

> Have you ever seen an artist shape a beautiful sculpture from a bar of gold or silver by beating alone? Hardly. To rightly form the bar, he now presses and hammers it carefully with his instruments, now smooths and polishes it with gentle yielding. If you would shape your boys to praiseworthy conduct, you must likewise offer them the helpful soothing of fatherly gentleness along with the pressure of correction. (as quoted in Grün, 9)

Anyone who raises children and young people has a position of leadership. This leadership will consist essentially in awakening life in these children, and in promoting in them the joy of growing into the unique image of God with which God has already imbued them.

HOSPITALITY

The guests for whom the cellarer is supposed to care are not the honorees or high clergy who let themselves be spoiled by monastery hospitality. Benedict is referring to the guests who have no rights, who can also be tedious: guests who need help, sick people longing for attention, people who ask boring questions that may well become uncomfortable. Today, certainly, the word refers also to asylum seekers and immigrants, who are often pushed away. A monastery should be open to such people, as well.

To Benedict, hospitality is an important value. The cellarer must constantly consider what true hospitality might look like today, so that it can be put into practice as Benedict intended: So that those who have no rights or home, those who have no place to go, those on the margins can find a place where they are allowed to be as they are, where they are respected and honored as human beings.

What is true of the monastery would also be a worthwhile task for any company. Every company today should practice hospitality. If a company integrates foreign workers into its staff, if it respects their dignity, it gives them a piece of home, practicing true hospitality. And this hospitality affects the world beyond the company. In the environment of such a company, immigrants will no longer feel themselves as strangers, but will feel accepted and included.

RESPONSIBILITY BEFORE GOD

To Benedict, leadership consists above all of taking responsibility for human beings, serving them, awakening life in them. Benedict reminds the cellarer that he will have to account for his actions on behalf of all these people on the day of judgment. The cellarer should be conscious of the responsibility he has taken on, his responsibility for the sick and the unprotected. His aim must not be to fulfill his duties well and look good in the eyes of others, but to fulfill his responsibilities before God.

What is most important is that he looks good to God. He is responsible before God for how he has treated people: whether he has served them and awakened life in them, or whether he has made them downcast and paralyzed, and deadened them. Many of today's managers complain about how difficult their employees are and about the burden of leading them. In his leadership seminar, Fritz Schürmeyer repeatedly emphasizes that such complaints are only confessions of a lack of leadership. If there are no problems, there would be no need for a leader. It is precisely the leader's role to face up to the problems, take responsibility for them, and solve them.

Benedict does not allow the cellarer or the abbot to complain about how difficult the community is. He reminds them of their responsibility for awakening life especially in those confreres who appear difficult. I personally know only too well that that is not always easy. And sometimes, I can recognize the resignation: "Oh, let them take one another apart with their own problems." But I can also feel that such resignation is a denial of leadership. In such moments, I am shaken up by St. Benedict's admonition that I will have to account before God for those entrusted to me. It is a matter of my own spiritual life whether or not I choose to lead.

MANAGEMENT
OF MATERIAL POSSESSIONS

After elaborating on leadership as a service to other people, Benedict discusses the cellarer's management of material possessions:

All the utensils of the monastery and, in fact, everything that belongs to the monastery should be cared for as though they were the sacred vessels of the altar. There must be no negligence on the part of the cellarer, nor any tendency to avarice nor to prodigality, nor wastefulness with the goods of the monastery. The administration should be carried out in all respects with moderation and in accordance with the instructions of the abbot or abbess. (*Rule*, 31:10–12)

REVERENCE FOR POSSESSIONS

In the passage quoted above, Benedict is making an allusion to a saying of the prophet Zechariah:

On that day there shall be inscribed on the bells of the horses, "Holy to the Lord." And the cooking pots in the house of the Lord shall

be as holy as the bowls in front of the altar;
and every cooking pot in Jerusalem and Judah
shall be sacred to the LORD of hosts. (Zechariah
14:20f)

Benedict interprets this prophecy of the end
of the distinction between sacred and profane as
applying to the monastery: the cellarer should not
distinguish between the tools and instruments of
the monastery (the Latin *vasa* refers to equipment,
dishes, agrarian tools, furniture, etc.) and its
financial assets (*substantia* refers to owned property,
money, possessions).

Here again, we see Benedict understanding
the service of leadership as a spiritual task, an
ecclesiastical act. Careful, mindful management
of worldly goods and possessions is like holding a
service at the altar. All the monastery's possessions,
whether they are dinner plates or machines
needed in the fields, should be treated with the
same reverence as altarpieces. All equipment is
a gift of God, and all possessions are filled with
God's goodness and wisdom. Even a monastery's
financial assets (*substantia*) are not external. It is
not a question of amassing and hoarding as much
money as possible. Instead, it is about recognizing
that everything the monastery has belongs to God.
Therefore, the cellarer must manage it carefully and
reverently.

Ownership is not rejected. Benedict is not advocating poverty as the ideal state in life. His goal is to cultivate mindfulness for the things God has given us. The purpose of our possessions is to give us inner peace. But possessions can also possess us if we become obsessed with increasing what we have. Then greed and covetousness take hold of us—and the early monks rightly saw these as one of the three fundamental vices.

Rather than greed, we should practice reverence for what we have, especially for the things that belong to the monastery. This reverence puts our avarice in perspective. Reverence asks us to engage in careful management, not greedy or miserly behavior. Reverence for what we have comes from the contemplation of the creation as described by Evagrius Ponticus. Part of this contemplation involves seeing things as they truly are, recognizing God in everything as the principal, primeval foundation. And contemplation involves using care when I handle material possessions. In them, in the end, I am touching God himself, whose spirit permeates all things.

SPIRITUAL USE OF PROPERTY

Benedict shows us specifically how the cellarer should manage the monastery's worldly possessions by the verbs he uses: The cellarer must not neglect (*neglere*) anything—there must be no negligence. The original Latin word *neglere* refers to a refusal to collect or read. But it also means to fail to pay attention to something. Neglect means dealing uncaringly with things. The cellarer should exercise care for all the monastery's property, including its financial assets. I often find it painful to watch how irresponsibly those in the Church and in ecclesiastical organizations deal with their money, how they fail to consider how they might increase their assets. Often, fear and false moralizing play an important role here.

Benedict's handling of money and property is free of such fearful moralizing. He sees God's work in everything—and their financial assets are likewise something with which the monks have been entrusted by God. For that reason, they must deal with them carefully and mindfully. They must not, however, become miserly. Miserliness comes from greed. A miser is always someone who is greedy for money, who can never have enough, who holds on to everything and clings to his worldly possessions. Proper disposition of one's assets also means sharing one's wealth with the poor, expending it in the service of others rather than hoarding it for oneself. But the cellarer must not waste or foolishly spend money. He should keep a measured approach to all things; he should do everything *commensurate*, that is, in a well-measured way, to an appropriate degree, in moderation.

This is especially important in decisions relating to money, because money tends to take possession of us entirely. Either we throw the money out the window as a way of boasting, or we sit on it and fearfully hold on to it. We would surely be acting in the spirit of Benedict if we considered what spiritual management of money would look like nowadays.

Especially in monasteries, I often witness a wholly "unspiritual" way of handling money. Money is used to exercise power. People are made dependent on the finances of the cellarer and must humbly implore the cellarer for money. Those the cellarer dislikes are always told: "We have no money; we need to save." And those who curry favor with the cellarer get what they want and more. Money is also used to signal status. Expensive new buildings are endowed, and more money is spent than necessary simply to look good to others. In those situations, money serves one's own prestige. Because one is not grounded in God, one feels a need to prove oneself through economic success and boast through financial largesse.

Others are afraid of losing money, and they structure their finances in ways that may be utterly secure but do not profit anyone. If we want to make more money, we must face the risk of losing money. This is the wisdom Jesus is invoking in the parable of the talents: The first two servants, who have increased the money given to them, are praised, while the third servant, who from fear has simply buried his talents, is cast out (cf. Matthew 25:14–30). Only those willing to take a risk can win. Those who bury their money are expressing their distrust of God, their own overattachment to faultlessness and perfection.

Jesus does not praise the success of the first two servants, he praises their trust. Trust in financial matters, to me, is a mark of truly spiritual financial management. Trust here means the willingness to risk without going too far. Whenever someone is successful in their financial dealings, they are apt to become overconfident and risk too much. Risk becomes like a current that pulls them under.

I have experienced those who are only concerned with their money as hollow and empty. Any person who is consumed with the thought of increasing their wealth is burying essential aspects of their humanity. I can feel that I do not enjoy conversations with such people. They project something unpleasant.

I have also witnessed some in the Church who mask their fear of risk with moralistic demands to invest money only where one can be sure that it will be handled properly. Certainly, business ethics are important in financial matters. I need to think very carefully about where and how I invest money. But I also see the danger of demonizing money, and of immediately casting aspersions of money-laundering or unethical conduct on all banks. But unless we actually invest the money ourselves, the banks will have that much more freedom to use our money in their own interests.

Some people give the impression that they are rebelling against the fact that money, interest rates, and stocks and shares exist at all. Part of accepting God's world is also affirming economic connections: only if I honor them as legitimate can I change them for the better. If I keep myself out of all these processes in order to maintain a "spotless record," I make myself especially culpable— because then, my lack of trust will come at a cost to others. I will overtax my colleagues and pile more and more work on them.

It is easy to sense how those who rigorously demand faultlessly ethical investment also let perfectionism creep into their expectations of colleagues. They hardly notice how they—while abhorring all power—are subconsciously exercising power of the kind that oppresses rather than supports. They make great demands on their colleagues, and when it comes to their own needs, they tend not to be too humble. In those cases, one can feel their shadow asserting itself and sowing trouble.

By investing my money meaningfully, I can take strain off my colleagues and create a healthy working environment in which we can work more effectively than under the pressure of financial hardship. For this reason, I always see truly spiritual money management as a service to the people around me, and as care for others.

In his book *A Global Ethic for Global Politics and Economics*, the late Hans Küng calls for Christian theologians not to act as an economically starry-eyed hive mind, seeking to fight social injustices by religiously elevating poverty and discrediting wealth wholesale. This is especially worrisome in the case of overly pious fanatics, who are using their vociferousness to mask a basic lack of economic comprehension and who almost never practice the ideas they preach (cf. Küng, 237). Of course, we should let our economic actions be guided by ethical principles. But Küng rightly points out that moralistic demands with no basis in economic reality are not actually ethical but sentimental, wishful thinking with a greater or lesser dose of piety.

Benedict, on the other hand, does not moralize. He accepts the need for economic networks while showing up a way to deal spiritually in this world with money and possessions. To me, that seems a more practicable route than romantically valorizing poverty. As a cellarer, I have often witnessed how those who most ardently extol poverty are for the most part personally very demanding and expect more than those who sensibly commit themselves to improving economic practices.

I will only begin to recognize what appropriate ethical yardsticks may be, once I make an effort to more precisely understand economic processes. We should certainly support ethical investment funds, as this support can encourage some companies to live up to ethical principles. Ethical investment funds, for example, have generally paid significantly higher dividends than eco-funds, which frequently invest in companies that work toward environmental protection but may treat their own employees harshly.

Business ethics guidelines must involve all aspects of human life: environmental policy, company structure, communication practices, respect for individual employees, treatment of rivals and suppliers. It is interesting to note that BMW fulfills these measures, while Volkswagen and the Swiss pharmaceutical giants Roche and Novartis currently do not.

Another current leadership strategy is saving money. It is certainly sensible not to waste the resources of our world. In today's society of excess and consumerism, thriftiness has become vital in order that future generations will still find a world worth living in. But when these money-saving measures come at a cost to human lives, such as is happening in healthcare or in education, I find that irresponsible. It is possible to "save oneself to death." To me, that kind of saving shows a lack of imagination. If I want, I can earn money in a meaningful way. I just need to use my imagination and develop new models for making money. Making money off others neither is creative nor does it yield long-term success. But a person who uses their money creatively will do damage to no one.

Instead, all will profit from their work. A person who makes his money at a cost to others, or who is merely trying to triumph over rivals, is not really leading. He needs others to lose out so that he can feel himself a winner. The art of true leadership, to me, is winning without anyone else losing.

> Competition as rivalry . . . leads to stress and burnout and is a primary cause of the malaise afflicting people and their organizations today. Antagonistic competition causes anxiety, poisons relationships, and is inherently toxic. There is no healthy destructive competition— in the end, it kills the victim as well as the perpetrator. (Secretan, 147)

Spiritual handling of money, as Benedict describes it in his sentence about the sacred altar vessels, is made up of three components.

1. Using money to serve others

Money should serve people, not the other way around. I must not use money to exercise power but must use money to give people opportunities to develop their skills and capabilities. In my dreams, money generally symbolizes my own abilities, strengths, and potential. I am using my money spiritually if I am using it to give people the chance to do meaningful work, if I enable them to grow and develop, to fulfill their own potential, and if I am also giving them enough space to recuperate from their work.

To me, a spiritual approach to money consists of serving others and awakening joy for life in them. Whenever everything depends on money, whenever people are overwhelmed by their inability to make ends meet, whenever people are ruled by money, money is being handled in an unspiritual way. Human beings must be the focal point, not money.

2. Freedom with respect to money

A spiritual attitude toward money shows itself in the freedom I have with respect to money. I must engage with money, but I must also let it go again and again. I cannot let myself be occupied by it. Money can ruin the soul. Money can make us blind to the true values of life. Money can make us hide behind a mask. In those cases, money is being used to compensate for a low sense of self-worth: hiding behind money in order to avoid facing up to the truth of my life. I must recognize all these dangers of money and make myself free from them. I can handle money spiritually only if I have grappled with my passions and am no longer ruled by the greed and covetousness that are probably within every human being.

To Benedict, spiritual management of finances consists largely of acting in an appropriate measure, or degree. I must consider how to invest the money well—but I must not do all that is possible. I must consciously set myself limits. And I must let go again of money. If I find myself thinking of financial questions repeatedly during prayer, for example, that is a sure sign that it is taking up too much space within me. Choosing to take a risk and then leaving up to God what will become of that risk—to me, that is an expression of inner freedom with respect to money. And we can only manage money spiritually if we have attained inner freedom from it, if we refuse to let it rule us.

3. Creative use of money

Spiritual management of money, to me, also means that I deal creatively with money: that I can trust enough to risk something without going too far. And an imaginative use of money, in my view, includes making use of the many different possibilities for earning money.

For example, I may earn money through manufacturing processes that react to what people need. In that case, I need to continually reconsider whether my company (or my monastery) is still producing what people actually need and what genuinely helps them. Production should never artificially create needs but should serve the people by helping them meet their true needs.

Another way of earning money is through creative use of the money itself. I might, for example, leverage the currency or interest rate situation, such as by buying cheap loans in the European market— Swiss francs or Japanese yen—and invest them more profitably, such as in foreign bonds, or in dollars, or in rand. Some moralists decry this idea, but it is typical winning without anyone's loss. Because when I purchase a cheap loan, it is in countries that have too much money. And then I invest it at a higher interest rate in countries where money is needed. This helps both parties. For example, in 1996, Argentina had to pay interest rates of eleven per cent, because investment there was deemed too risky. Today, that rate has decreased to seven per cent. If in 1996, therefore, I had purchased an Argentinian bond at an interest rate of 11.75 %, I did not harm the country, but actually helped it in the long term: today, its economy is doing better.

One can use the differential in the loan and bond interest rates to support projects that do not of themselves make a profit, such as a school, teacher training, or development projects in the Third World. I see this as a creative use of money: instead of complaining about the lack of money, I can look for ways of earning it. Of course, it would be wrong to think that "the sky is the limit" here.

It requires patience and the necessary humility to understand that one cannot achieve everything one wants. But I view the avoidance of such strategies out of fear of risk, with the result that one must beg others for money, as an unspiritual way of managing money. Creative use of money means influencing the economic situation in the world. And that means investing in companies that have a vision for the future and that practice ethical principles.

I can affect economic processes positively only by moving the needle with my own financial dealings. If I switch to moralizing, I look for scapegoats everywhere in order to prove my own innocence. But that supposed faultlessness is exactly what makes me culpable.

ENCOUNTERING OTHERS

Benedict continues his instructions to the cellarer:

 Among the most important qualities the cellarer needs to cultivate is humility and the ability to give a pleasant answer even when a request must be refused. Remember how scripture says that a kindly word is of greater value than a gift, however precious. Although the cellarer's responsibility embraces all that is delegated by the superior, there must be no attempt to include what the superior has forbidden. The members of the community should receive their allotted food without any self-important fuss or delay on the part of the cellarer which might provoke them to resentment. The cellarer should remember what is deserved, according to the Lord's saying, by those who provoke to sin one of his little ones. (*Rule*, 31:13–16)

A KINDLY WORD

If care and mindfulness are the most important virtues in managing material possessions, Benedict demands humility above all for interactions with others. This humility does not mean making oneself small or obsequious. Rather, *humilitas* is the courage to face up one's own humanity and earthly nature. A leader should always remember that he too is only a human, that he is of the earth and has earth-bound needs.

A person who knows his own shadow and imperfections will never place himself above others. He will not judge them harshly. He will not judge them at all. He will try to deal with others in the same way as he deals with himself:

> In everything do to others as you would have them do to you. (Matthew 7:12)

This golden rule becomes the yardstick of his actions. He will treat others as he expects to be treated. Across all religions, the golden rule is seen as a maxim of human interaction. It has even become a generally accepted premise of appropriate economic ethics and fair business practices.

Humility—as the courage to face up to one's own humility—leads to reverence for and friendliness toward human beings. Benedict specifies what he has already mentioned before: The cellarer cannot fulfill all the wishes that brothers have of him. He is subject to limited resources. But a kindly word (*sermo responsionis bonus*) is limitless and can be given to all.

A story of the early monks relates how a young monk insulted a heathen priest. The priest retaliated by beating him to death. When a wise and old monk encountered the same priest, the monk spoke to him with kindness. The priest was so astonished that he followed the old monk and became his student. The story closes with the beautiful words:

> A cruel word makes even the kind cruel; a kind word makes even the cruel kind.

Words can change people. An ill-spoken word can make us ill; words that put us down cause us to feel a sense of worthlessness. Words can paralyze or liberate, can push down or raise up, can dishearten or encourage, hurt or heal, deaden or awaken life. The cellarer must therefore exercise great care with respect to his words. He should not answer out of disappointment or anger, but always with a good word—a word that is a true answer because it actually engages with the person who has asked.

Some people in positions of leadership do not listen properly. They do not engage with the problems of the person who has come to them, but only use them as a springboard to talk about themselves and their own problems. The result is that they use words that do not uplift, but rather, oppress. Benedict expects the cellarer, as a manager, to awaken the good in others through his good words. Benedict is referring to the Epistle to the Ephesians:

> Let no evil talk come out of your mouths, but only what is useful for building up, as there is need, so that your words may give grace to those who hear. (Ephesians 4:29)

The kind word is supposed to build up human lives, not tear people down. It is supposed to uplift the listener, not bring him low.

Building means to make grow, to develop, to shape into being. A word that builds up allows a human being to grow. A person can blossom through the good word they receive, can grow into the image God has made of them and will find space in that image to live. One can live in a kind word as in a house, can feel at home there. A kind word is a healing space for the person who hears it.

Ephesians also states, as a second effect of a kindly word, that it is supposed to give grace (*kharin didonai*) to the hearer. The hearer should be given the gift of grace, attention, tenderness, love. In that word, my love reaches the other and puts him in contact with the love that slumbers in his heart, waiting only to be awakened by a kind word.

The statement that a kind word is to be ranked above a gift refers to a verse in the Wisdom of Sirach:

Indeed, does not a word surpass a good gift?
Both are to be found in a gracious person.
(Sirach 18:17)

Benedict is drawing on the wisdom of the biblical Book of Ecclesiasticus, also known as the Wisdom of Sirach, which brings together insights from the Jewish tradition and Hellenistic philosophy. The sayings collected there could be taken up by any other religion. They express experiences that are universal to people all across the earth. Benedict is showing the openness of his heart by referring to a spiritual tradition that connects all human beings.

When dealing with his confreres, the cellarer is supposed to pay attention to his words. Many managers speak without thinking. They are constantly berating those who work for them and creating a poor work environment. They are committing spiritual pollution: everyone must then fear that the boss is going to talk about them just as he talks about all their co-workers.

Other bosses respond to their employees with sarcasm or cynicism, discouraging or criticizing them. Some people are incapable of appreciation and can only see the negative sides of others. They do not give their co-workers a friendly greeting when they enter the office, but immediately discover something that has gone wrong. Perhaps there is a document on the desk that should not be there, or a business letter has been poorly phrased. These kinds of managers are fixated on the negative and will therefore inevitably project negativity.

Ephesians cautions against speaking about impurity and sin, on the premise that sinful words corrupt; such words can provoke decay. A good, kindly word, however, calls out the good in a person. It makes it easier to believe the good. We feel good when we hear kind words, better able to accept ourselves, in a better mood. And this better mood, these raised spirits, help us do good work. Anyone who wants to lead others must first master the art of praise. Praise, after all, means to speak well of, or to say good things to a person: *bene-dicere*. If we address the good in a person, we will awaken that good in them and bring it to the surface. This will motivate any employee far better than criticism or control.

Today, many managers believe that above all, they must have control of their employees. But anyone who seeks control will inevitably find their organization slipping from their control, simply because a person who is too tightly controlled will develop resistance. A person oppressed by control will start to use their energy to circumvent that control.

Control may prevent mistakes, but it does not awaken life. A kindly word, on the other hand, can bring employees to life. Ephesians focuses on two effects of a good word: it builds up, and it offers grace and tenderness. A good word not only builds up an employee but also contributes to the building of a healthy workplace environment and a successful company. It is like a foundation on which a business can build. Kind words are a sign of attention, of tender care for each individual. A person who has received such care can also turn to their work with their whole heart. If we experience rejection, we turn away not only from other people who may reject or have rejected us, but from our work as well. We are too caught up in the hurt to be able to engage with our work.

RESPECTING BOUNDARIES

Benedict's next observation suggests that Benedict himself had negative experiences with a monastery administrator: Benedict admonishes the cellarer that he must not extend his purview beyond what the abbot has entrusted to him. He should not involve himself in everything. There are managers who do stick their nose into everything. They believe that they are in charge of everything. Not content with their own task, they take it upon themselves to offer their opinions on every aspect of the company and to intrude on other's competencies. By doing this, they create only disorder.

Benedict explicitly states that the cellarer should still see the whole picture: He must always fulfill his task with reference to the framework of the entire monastery. He is meant to look beyond the end of his nose. But he must not involve himself in everything or form a counter-administration.

In many companies, department heads build up an in-house power base that they extend into all other departments. They eagerly collect information from other departments in order to exploit this information against their rivals at opportune moments. They pull hidden strings and exert influence everywhere. This blocks effective work.

A leader must also be able to let go. He must be content with the tasks set before him. If he completes them well, he contributes to building up the entire company. But if he constantly takes a hand in the work of others, he is only throwing a wrench into the machinery. And all too often, he will try to draw attention away from his own mistakes by calling out other departments on their imperfections.

PASSING ON INFORMATION

The cellarer is also supposed to give his confreres their measure of food and drink regularly and without delay or high-handedness that might lead to resentment. Today, the "allotted food" represents appropriate payment that a company gives its employees. But it can also represent the information that a boss must pass on, the interaction and engagement he owes those who work for him. Listening and earnest interest, respect and discretion, the attention and care a manager gives his employees—all these things nourish them. And only a leadership style that nourishes the people it leads rather than exploiting them is sustainable.

Today, simple civility and kindness are being rediscovered as important aspects of leadership.

> When there is a decline in civility, the toxicity within organizations increases and the soul shrivels. Civility is one of the most effective antidotes to this toxicity; civilized behavior is soothing to the soul. (Secretan, 73)

Employees expect their superiors to take them seriously, to listen when they describe their problems, to honor their dignity and care about how they are doing.

SHOWING APPRECIATION

It is therefore essential that a leader never be high-handed to those he is leading. He must never set himself above others or let them feel that he is better than they are. He should not wield his power, but rather speak levelly with them, eye-to-eye, in order to show that he appreciates them. Once again, humility, rather than high-handedness, is called for.

But a high-handed manager sets himself above others, he "sticks his nose in the air," becomes "stuck up." Many employees feel unappreciated, put down, even humiliated by their bosses. This paralyzes them and creates resentment in the form of powerless anger. This mute anger blocks cooperation and takes up unnecessary energy, which the company can then no longer harness. One way of looking down on one's employees, for example, is to make them wait. Punctuality is the courtesy of kings, a proverb tells us. A king does not keep his subjects waiting. He honors them by keeping to the appointed time.

Many of today's managers seem to have lost this virtue. They show their importance by letting their employees wait for them for as long as possible. Some politicians come late on principle, just like some bishops or executives. There are particularly unfair methods of keeping others waiting and then even watching them via video cameras. A CEO, for example, can create great tension by keeping his department heads waiting in a conference room for a long time. He can observe who is accepting and who rebels—who dares criticize the boss. And the waiting tires out his colleagues and makes it easier for him to get his way. But such an unfair method of working will not pay for long. Soon, disrespect to the employees will lead them, in turn, to disrespect their boss—he may be feared, but he will not be respected. The aggression he sends out will be turned against him, and the tiniest mistake will make his job insecure. Not without reason does Benedict say of abbots that "they should seek to be loved more than they are feared" (*Rule*, 64:15). A leader who rules by fear paralyzes those he leads. Only a boss who is loved will find that employees come through for him. A feared boss, on the other hand, soon finds out that no one has his back.

NOT UPSETTING OTHERS

The cellarer should not provoke resentment in his confreres, should not upset them (*nonscandalizentur*). Benedict then refers to an admonition from the community rule as set out in chapter 18 of the Gospel of Matthew:

If any of you put a stumbling block before one of these little ones who believe in me, it would be better for you if a great millstone were fastened around your neck and you were drowned in the depth of the sea. (Matthew 18:6)

By "little ones," Matthew means simple, honest Christians—the normal people and colleagues who do not have anyone to advocate for their needs. A manager must give these employees the same respect and appreciation as he gives those who are higher up in the hierarchy of the company.

The Latin word for upsetting is *scandalizo*. It literally means to set a trap. When a cellarer lets his confreres wait or looks down on them, he is setting a trap, baiting them to fall into the trap of anger. And in this way, he is wielding his power over them. After all, if I upset a person, I have taken control of their mood, and they think of me for the rest of the day.

Some managers find it satisfying to upset their colleagues this way, to exercise their power. By letting their colleagues or even their customers wait, they are communicating that it is actually an honor that they have even taken the time. But in the person who is kept waiting, this behavior creates either impotent rage, resignation, or a feeling of dependency. This waiting not only wastes valuable time, but also decreases employees' motivation to use their time effectively for the good of the company. And such behavior is contagious: Soon every department is keeping the others waiting, showing its power.

Then there are those who come late to joint meetings in order to draw all the attention on themselves. This is also a trap. A good manager will see through this trap and avoid it by starting the meeting on time. That way, the person who comes late has only themselves to blame. The group does not give them the power to hold up the entire meeting. But employees have very little recourse against a boss who keeps them waiting. For this reason, it is deeply unfair to upset them by keeping them waiting, and thus setting traps for them that keep them ensnared in impotent rage.

GIVING THE SOUL WINGS

In his chapter on the abbot or abbess, Benedict elaborates his thinking on leadership as given in the chapter on the cellarer, revealing the full wisdom of his philosophy of leading human beings. For this reason, I will cite several verses on interpersonal leadership from that chapter, to supplement the leadership principles from the chapter on the cellarer.

[The abbot or abbess] should reflect on what a difficult and demanding task they have accepted, namely, that of guiding souls and serving the needs of so many different characters; gentle encouragement will be needed for one, strong rebukes for another, rational persuasion for another, according to the character and intelligence of each. It is the task of the superiors to adapt with sympathetic understanding to the needs of each so that they may not only avoid any loss but even have the joy of increasing the number of good sheep in the flock committed to them.

It is above all important that monastic superiors should not underrate or think lightly of the salvation of the souls committed to them by giving too much attention to transient affairs of this world which have no lasting value. They should remember always that the responsibility they have undertaken is that of guiding souls and that they will have to render an account of the guidance they have given. Negligence in this responsibility cannot be excused by the demands made on them because of the slender resources of the monastery. They should remember this saying from scripture: Seek first the kingdom of God and his righteousness and all these things will be given to you also; then also there is the text: Nothing is lacking for those who fear him. (*Rule*, 2:31–36)

Leadership requires a profound knowledge of human nature—and a great deal of flexibility. To Benedict, leadership consists of "guiding souls" (*regere animas*). It is not a question of pushing people back and forth like pieces on a board, not a question of utilizing them as labor machines, but of doing justice to their souls. Guiding a soul involves paying attention to a person's interior life, that I care for the unique, primeval image of them that God has made for himself. A leader is supposed to interact with a person in such a way that that person can fulfill their own deeply personal image and live in the way God has entrusted to them.

Real leadership consists of addressing the soul of a person and giving it wings. When leadership suppresses or ignores the soul of a person, it is cutting that person off from their inner source, their inner well-spring of creativity, imagination, and joy in their work. Addressing the soul means making a space for creativity, a "Sanctuary," in the words of Lance Secretan:

> Leaders who seek to liberate the soul through creativity must establish a Sanctuary in which failure is not punished but valued as a learning experience. (Secretan, 181)

As an example, Secretan gives the story of Chrysler, the auto manufacturer. Its chairman, Lee Iacocca, supported Hal Sperlich, the inventor of the minivan, enabling him to turn his ideas into reality. For ten years, Sperlich had tried unsuccessfully to convince Chrysler's rival Ford of the new concept. But when Iacocca hired him at Chrysler and supported him, Sperlich generated such an explosion of innovation that the company flourished and its stock soared. Nourishing the soul, in the end, brought the company greater profits than any previous business strategy built on caution and precise cost calculations.

GROWING LIFE

Benedict expects the abbot to serve the individual characters of his many different monks, to engage with each of them individually. To me, leadership means meditating on the individual, considering his or her potential, limitations, and weak points, considering what might support or hinder him or her.

For example, the abbot should adapt his behavior to the character and intelligence of the individual, with the goal that both the individual and the community can grow. Benedict here uses the word *augmentatio* to show what he means by authority. Authority comes from the Latin *augere*, meaning "to increase, or grow." The abbot should increase the growth and development of each individual, should strengthen life in the individual and the community simultaneously. Our abbot in Münsterschwarzach is very dedicated to making sure that everyone receives good education and continual professional development. This introduces new ideas into the community and, in the long run, is financially lucrative. Unfortunately, not all monasteries fulfill these ideals. In some monasteries, superiors try to use confreres to "fill holes" instead of looking to their growth. Their growth would involve giving them enough space to keep learning and developing themselves, as well as creating for them an atmosphere in which they can make the best use of their abilities and skills. In the long run, this will be of use to the community, as well.

Of course, this does not mean that the individual should think only of themselves. The ideas of increase, development, and growth only have meaning if we grow together, if individual growth is in the service of everyone.

VALUING THE INDIVIDUAL

In Benedict's view, the individual human being is more important than economic success. Organizations often put their success above their workers. Benedict, however, admonishes the abbot not to let the monastery's slender resources ever become a reason to overwork its members or to ignore the salvation of their souls (*salus animarum*). The well-being, the unity, the wholeness of the individual is more important to Benedict than wealth. I often see monasteries overwork their members with the justification of insufficient resources. Everyone must work more, so that the monastery can be economically successful. But this negligence of each individual does not lead to economic success. Quite the contrary: Because every individual is overwhelmed with work, there is no way to create a long-term, sustainable, healthy financial basis, either.

Here, too, the spiritual foundation of leadership and economic business emerges clearly. If the abbot seeks above all for the kingdom of God, he will also manage the economic side of the monastery well; everything else will be given to him. This is not a cheap answer. Instead, it is borne out by experience. A person who truly seeks God will also encounter the world appropriately. By fearing God, we engage more mindfully with those around us, and then we will not suffer lack. If an organization or a community has a joint goal that motivates them, they will develop ideas for how to work successfully economically. But pressure and moralizing about the need for everyone to work more so that the community can survive is not an effective leadership strategy for the long term.

LOVE AND MODERATION

In a later chapter, too, Benedict focuses on the primacy of the individual human being above all the economic goals, ideas, and ideologies we so often subject ourselves to or force ourselves into. He says of the abbot:

While they must hate all vice, they must love their brothers or sisters. In correcting faults, they must act with prudence, being conscious of the danger of breaking the vessel itself by attacking the rust too vigorously. They should always bear their own frailty in mind and remember not to crush the bruised reed. Of course, I do not mean that they should allow vices to grow wild but rather use prudence and charity in cutting them out, so as to help each one in their individual needs, as I have already said. They should seek to be loved more than they are feared.

They should not be troublemakers nor given to excessive anxiety, nor should they be too demanding or obstinate, nor yet interfering and full of suspicion so as never to be at rest. In making decisions, they should use foresight and care in analyzing the situation, so that whether they are giving orders about sacred or about secular affairs, they should be farseeing and moderate in their decisions. They should reflect on the discretion of the holy patriarch Jacob when he said: If I force my flock to struggle further on their feet, they will all die in a single day. They should take to heart these and other examples of discretion, the mother of virtues, and manage everything in the monastery so that the strong may have ideals to inspire them and the weak may not

be frightened away by excessive demands.
(*Rule*, 64:11–19)

These are important foundational principles
for leading fellow human beings. The first is
the statement, which Benedict formulates with
reference to St. Augustine, that an abbot should
hate vice but love his brethren—sometimes phrased
as "hate the sin, love the sinner." This does not
mean a *laissez-faire* style of leadership, which would
be weakness. But the abbot must make a clear
distinction between person and behavior, between
what is wrong and the person who has been ruled by
the mechanisms of evil and let themselves be pulled
in the wrong direction. Throughout all correction,
the leader must always love those he corrects. He
must trust them to have good intentions and have
erred unwillingly.

But love alone does not produce good leadership.
It must be combined with intelligence. The abbot
must not do too much of a good thing. The Roman
playwright Terence's maxim of *ne quid nimis*, or
nothing in excess, has long become a common
nugget of wisdom. And the leader needs this
common wisdom—it is common sense that excess
is not good for us.

Monks say that all excess comes from demons:
By over-improving, we make things worse; by
overcorrecting, we can hurt others. Psychologists
such as Paul Watzlawick spoke of the attitude

of "more of the same" as doing more harm than good. If I keep demanding more and more—better performance, faster turn-around, higher output, increased revenue—then the result will eventually be total collapse.

HEALING

Benedict then offers the metaphor of a vessel which breaks if one too eagerly removes the rust. Benedict links this proverbial image with the biblical metaphor that Matthew cites from the book of Isaiah to describe Jesus's actions. Jesus's many acts of healing fulfill what Isaiah prophesied of the Messiah:

> He will not break a bruised reed or quench a smoldering wick. (Matthew 12:20)

The abbot is being compared to Jesus the healer, Jesus who helps others out of their illness. Leadership has a great deal to do with healing. A person who leads others must lead them to their own health and well-being, must lead in such a way that others find their own wholeness and can give up their inner conflicts. A leader must lead others to live and work as whole individuals in a community.

The comparison between a leader and Jesus reveals a deep premise of Benedict's model of leadership: like Jesus, the leader must uplift his charges, must encourage and heal them. Healing and leadership, here, are seen as linked. This is a tall order. And yet, the way a person leads projects a great deal into the lives of those led—either things that sicken them, or things that heal; either things that humiliate, or things that uplift.

According to Benedict, the last responsibility of a manager is that he should heal those working under him. He may heal by giving them work that sparks in them joy in life. Work that gives us joy can have a healing effect not just on our soul, but on our body, as well. And that healing can also occur if the boss respects his employees, takes their hurt seriously rather than probing their wounds, puts himself in the shoes of every individual, and considers what might serve that person's life. By awakening life and communicating joy in life, he has just as much healing power as a doctor who searches for the correct diagnosis and offers the appropriate medicine. A healthy work environment, based on sound leadership, can be a healing balm for the many wounds we all bring to work with us. Disrespect and hurt would keep reopening these wounds, and they would spread through the entire company like an infection.

A manager therefore has a great responsibility for the health and hurts of his employees.

CONFRONTING ONE'S OWN FRAILTY

Benedict also exhorts the abbot to bear his own frailty in mind at all times. Benedict knows all the stories of older, strict monks being too harsh with a younger monk struggling with his vows. The young monk is then plunged in despair—and it turns out that the person who berated him so harshly cannot himself fulfill what he demands of his younger charge. In fact, experience teaches us that those who moralize loudest never live out themselves what they demand of others. The leader, therefore, should look closely at his own conscience, whether he is actually putting into practice what he calls for or corrects in others.

Nowadays, there is often a large gulf between what managers expect of their employees and the lifestyle they themselves enjoy. But no boss can hide from his workers how he lives. The disparity between expectations and reality then disappoints and demotivates the workers. They are especially angry if a boss on the one hand asks every sacrifice of his employees and deals with them harshly while allowing himself every lenience and never following any moral precept.

When we look at most of those who deal so adamantly with others, we find that their strictness toward others is meant to distract from their own weaknesses. But if I bear in mind my own frailty (*fragilitas* also means inadequacy and inconstancy), I will deal more gently with colleagues who have made a mistake. I will not set myself above them. I know that I cannot guarantee my own infallibility, either.

But nor can I let everything go. I must not fall prey to pessimism, thinking that all people are fundamentally bad, or that entrenched patterns cannot be changed. Such complaints are unhelpful and only constitute an admission of a lack in leadership qualities.

ADDRESSING TRUTH

When, at the age of thirty-two, I was made cellarer, I had the impression that quite a few things in our monastery were so entrenched that nothing could be done about them. At the time, I spoke frequently with Father Richard, who had been a company director for many years before becoming a monk at age sixty-nine. He never accepted such complaints and always insisted that it must be a question of leadership. Leadership means active shaping, and leadership is primarily attentive care. If so many things are not well, it is a sign that workers feel neglected, that no one has truly cared about them. Benedict admonishes the cellarer not to give free reign to errors and failures. He should not offer any fertile ground to the vices (*vitium* means hurt, dishonor, mistake, badness) by building his power on intrigues or unsubstantiated rumor, or by setting his confreres against one another in order to look good by comparison.

If he nourished evil by agitating against his colleagues or spreading bad words about them, he would destroy the community. He would be causing a downward spiral. No one would put in effort, since it would not matter. The leader himself would be closing his eyes to reality. This kind of defeatist climate creates a downward pull that eventually sucks everyone in.

In some companies, I have encountered a morass of emotions and intrigues that will never yield anything good. Leadership means addressing mistakes and—as Benedict says—cutting them off, amputating them. He is interested in effective elimination of mistakes, not moralizing invective against all the things that are not working as they should. The abbot should address problems at their root, not just treat their symptoms, and he can do this only if he confronts the community with the truth about itself, if he helps the community jointly address the ways its members stand in conflict. Only by addressing and working through these misunderstandings and conflicts can a climate develop in which people are working together instead of against one another.

But such discussions and pruning away of mistakes and vices requires intelligence and love. Nowadays, many monastic communities—just like many companies—are incapable of openly discussing the true problems they have. They cannot talk candidly, intelligently, and lovingly about themselves and one another, but only aggressively and hurtfully. In this way, every individual falls back on themselves and tries to fight for themselves.

This is not a climate in which anything can grow. And especially in climates where there is no conversation, many people fall sick. Each leader, then, must have experience in group dynamics in order to support communication between his colleagues and lead them on the path toward communal healing and cleansing.

THINKING FROM THE HEART

In the brief passage I quoted above, Benedict twice demands that the abbot behave according to intelligence (*prudentia*). The word *prudentia* comes from the older *providentia*, which means farsightedness or foresight. An intelligent person looks beyond what catches their eye. They have a wide horizon. Their eyes are not fixated on their mistakes; instead, they see the mistakes in a larger context.

Intelligence involves looking at reality from all sides before calmly and rationally deciding what is right. It does not mean acting out of haste, but out of a considered calm. An intelligent person gives himself the time to listen to the arguments of the person he is correcting. He does not immediately judge, but first looks without judging at the whole picture. Intelligence originally means discernment, literally "reading between." Intelligence, then, involves a fine sensibility, the ability to distinguish between and to catch small differences. A rough person will see only the surface, but a discerning person will sense the context, the background, and the environment in which a mistake can occur.

An intelligent person will always also think with their heart—intelligence is always linked with love. In Antoine de Saint-Exupéry's famous *Little Prince*, the titular character tells us that it is only with the heart that one sees well. In order to love someone, I need to see the good in them and believe in the good in them—and I need to bring the good out into the world through praise.

By praising a person, I am calling out the good in them. If I am fixated only on negative things, I will be like someone who keeps trying to scratch off the rust without noticing that the vessel's wall is perilously thin and threatens to break at any moment.

FEAR DIVIDES—LOVE ENLIVENS

The idea that the abbot should work to be loved rather than feared is another reference to St. Augustine, whom Benedict evidently held in high esteem.

Some bosses think that they are effective only if every employee is afraid of them. But fear paralyzes. In a climate of fear new ideas cannot thrive, and truly creative and effective work becomes impossible. Every individual is busy making sure they do not make a single mistake. Fear divides rather than connects people. Fearful people orbit their own thoughts, trying to make themselves look as good as possible in order to avoid criticism. A fearful person will attribute all mistakes to others. This creates an environment of mistrust and mutual suspicion.

The widespread climate of workplace harassment we see in so many companies nowadays is, in the end, attributable to the leadership style prevalent in those companies. A boss who wants to be feared by his employees will spread a climate of fear and divisiveness. One worker will compete with another. The only cooperation becomes banding together against the weakest. The weakest becomes the scapegoat—but as soon as the scapegoat has been driven out, one needs the next scapegoat. This will never produce an environment in which anyone is happy to work. Every person lives in fear of becoming the next scapegoat and being hounded out. So, everyone conforms, in order not to draw attention. In such an environment, almost 80 percent of workers' energy is used for keeping up one's position. And then there is no more energy left for effective and creative work.

Where fear divides and paralyzes, love creates connection and a climate of joy in work. With his instruction that the abbot should work to be loved, Benedict is certainly not saying that the abbot should behave obsequiously and try to please everyone. That would be a sign of weakness. When employees sense that their superior is dependent on receiving love and admiration from them, they do not respect him.

Love and respect do go together. Only when a person is centered in themselves and not dependent on being loved by everyone can they be truly loved. If a manager lives out his need for love and appreciation in front of his employees, he must buy his love from them through preferment or concessions. Only if he is free, if he turns to his employees out of love for them, can they love him.

A person who gives love will receive love. A person who seeks to buy love will run after it in vain. In a climate of mutual love, all workers work for one another, not only for their superior, but for their coworker at the next cubicle, as well.

Love produces relationships of mutual community. And love awakens joy in work. A person who enjoys their work because they feel appreciated and loved there will take fewer sick days and approach their work with greater motivation. But no one enjoys working for a boss they fear, and will not work overtime, either. But for a boss who is loved, one does not check the clock. Instead, the work itself gives one wings.

ESCHEWING EXCESS

The negative behaviors and attitudes that Benedict wants the abbot to let go of correspond to those we encountered in the chapter on the cellarer: The abbot should not be fearful, because fearfulness creates a climate of fear.

Intriguing is Benedict's exhortation that the abbot should *non sit nimius*—literally, not be excessive. He should not exceed the appropriate measure, should not work too much, be too strict, too precise, or too quick. Excess of this kind is discouraging to those around him. They feel inferior. If a person lives one particular characteristic too completely, then the opposite of that characteristic is pushed into the shadows and will therefore affect the overall environment negatively. The abbot must find the right measure, the right degree in himself. He must remain balanced between the wide variety of his tendencies, emotions, and habits.

A leader who is himself extreme will tend to promote extreme behavior in others, and this will divide his colleagues. Too much on one side always comes at the cost of too little on the other. If we want to lead others, we must understand our inner contradictions and keep them in equilibrium.

AVOIDING ENVY AND SUSPICION

Benedict admonishes the abbot not to be envious or suspicious, because he would otherwise never find rest. When a manager is envious of those who are more skilled than he is, or of those who are more popular, he cannot accept others.

I know a director of a psychiatric clinic who is pathologically envious of all his best therapists. Whenever a therapist is more popular with patients than this director is, the director views that therapist as an antagonist. After all, the therapist is taking away some of the popularity the director wants only for himself.

A sister in a religious hospital once told me of a superior who rebuked her harshly whenever she was praised by the head doctor. This sister had to efface herself so that, whenever she was given outside praise, this superior would not put her down. The sister became paralyzed and demotivated by this. Worrying about her envious superior cost her more effort than working with the patients.

Such environments are not conducive to good work. This is not leadership but hindrance. An envious boss sucks up all the energy one has, and motivation plummets. One feels lifeless. The word *envy* comes from old Latin roots meaning to look maliciously upon, or to cast an evil eye. An envious person spreads malice, evil, and bitterness, which destroy the workplace environment and make co-workers sick. To lead others, one must be free of envy. Only then can one accept others and take joy in their work and presence.

It is similar with *suspicion*, which word has its roots in looking secretly at something or looking with mistrust. This reflects the experience of suspicion: I do not see the other person as they are but through the lens of my own mistrust. I see the other person filtered through pathological illusions. If I look at someone with suspicion, I will see ghosts everywhere. I will discover intrigues against me, rejection, criticism. And in trying to counteract them, I am tilting at windmills, fighting against my own diseased imagination. I am using my energy against myself.

These illusory battles take up a great deal of energy. Employees in some companies have told me that over a third of their workday is taken up by dealing with such mistrust, such illusory battles. They imagine what others think of them, and spend their time thinking about how to react to completely imagined thoughts others might have of them.

By constantly thinking about others' thoughts, a suspicious person keeps themselves from thinking clearly about their work. This blocks their work: They cannot commit to their work and organize it appropriately. Instead, everything becomes filtered through suspicion and mistrust. Work is misused as a way of reacting to the supposed thoughts of others, instead of being addressed on its objective terms.

When a leader is ruled by such thoughts of envy and mistrust, says Benedict, he will never find rest. Rest, evidently, is necessary for working well. If a manager lives in constant restlessness over the question of what disaster the employees will precipitate next, he will never complete the tasks actually in front of him. He will not lead the community, but infect others with his own restlessness, constantly throwing sand in the gears.

Some managers do not listen. Any request from an employee is seen as an affront to themselves. They do not listen to what the person is actually saying, but instead formulate their own theory as to what the other person is likely planning. Such a climate of suspicion and restlessness cannot yield anything positive. Colleagues feel the mistrust, feel that their superior is not free, is too self-involved to devote himself to them and their problems and look for appropriate solutions. And on top of that, the manager will overwhelm himself: His leadership position becomes too effortful, as he is fighting on all fronts simultaneously.

Other managers hide behind their own restlessness. They are constantly busy in order to avoid criticism. This gives the impression that while the manager may be sacrificing himself for everyone, he is overwhelmed and never comes to rest. No real leadership can come from such a state. At best, it creates pity in the workers. Or the manager will try to transfer his own restlessness to his employees by constantly assigning them new strategies. But it is soon clear to everyone that this constant change comes not from a clear vision but from personal restlessness. For this reason, all attempts at change fall flat.

DISCERNMENT AND TEMPERANCE

To Benedict, discretion—in Latin: *discretio*, or the ability to distinguish, discernment—is the mother of all virtues. Especially for an abbot, it is the precondition of wise, considered leadership.

In early monasticism, discernment and distinguishing were necessary abilities for spiritual companionship. This *discretio* is a gift of the Holy Spirit. It cannot merely be learned, but it is possible to practice it by observing one's own thoughts and emotions closely and learning to distinguish between them.

In the end, *discretio*, or discernment, refers to the ability to discern the difference between the spirits: Which is the Spirit of God and which is the ungodly spirit of this world? Which thought comes from God and which from my demons? To the monks, one important criterion of this discernment is that only those thoughts can come from God that cause a deep peace in the soul.

A person who can distinguish, who has discernment, can also decide. Such a person will make their decisions not according to some method or guideline, but based on their ability of discernment, their inner feeling for what is right. The best decisions are made not by processing all available information and considering countless arguments for each side, but by trusting one's intuition. A person who follows their intuition knows what is right. They may not be able to give a precise reason for why their decision is right. It has been made "from the gut," not the head. But they have an inner feeling for rightness. This is *discretio*.

Benedict also cites the example of Jacob, who did not want to overtax his flock so that they would survive. Here, the gift of discernment is paired not only with the decision not to continue walking beyond what the herd can take, but also with a sense of the right degree, with temperance.

Discretio, then, refers to both discernment and moderation. Especially in the immoderate times we live in, leadership that understands about temperance—the appropriate degree, moderation that is right for people—does us good. Only by maintaining temperance can we work effectively and well over the long term. A leader must never take the measure that is appropriate for him as the measure he forces on others. Some managers, for example, are always giving their employees the feeling that they work too little: These managers work ceaselessly and unconsciously communicate to their employees that the same is expected of them.

True leadership, however, means that I recognize and respect what each person's individual measure and individual boundaries are. I cannot discover what is right for others by not challenging them or leaving them alone. Instead, I must challenge them to discover the limits of what they can do—but when they reach that limit, I must respect it. Then I can consider with what I can entrust this person within their limits.

Many of today's employees, for fear of becoming overextended, set themselves too narrow limits. They box themselves in so that they face no danger of overexertion. But this is not satisfying either. I need to cross my limits at least once in order to know where they truly are. If I never even approach my limits, I will never know what I am capable of. Benedict connects discretion and temperance explicitly when he writes:

> They should take to heart these and other examples of discretion, the mother of virtues, and manage everything in the monastery so that the strong may have ideals to inspire them and the weak may not be frightened away by excessive demands. (*Rule*, 64:19)

Discernment is supposed to lead to the ability to organize and guide all things appropriately. Temperance, too, implies an order that is appropriate, that takes measure of a person and holds to that measure. *Temperare* comes from *tempus*, which refers to a stretch of sky, time, or time interval. To Benedict, leadership involves taking the appropriate measure, to let everything occur at the appropriate time in the appropriate moment.

JUSTICE BETWEEN THE STRONG AND THE WEAK

Leadership, as we saw above, also has to do with shaping and forming: I must form all things in the way in which they correspond best to reality. I must shape them into the form intended for them. *Temperare* also means to mitigate or alleviate. Benedict never sees leadership as something violent, but as something that makes mild, that softens, makes pliable enough to fit into the appropriate shape.

This mild shaping and forming does have strength and power. A plant that slowly grows into its intended form has incredible power as well. It can penetrate concrete and keep growing all the same. The strength of leadership also shows itself in the fact that those with strength in the community are challenged by the abbot. The goal of this is not to level out differences between the strong and the weak, but to do justice to both. The strong should find what they are looking for. They should find the challenge to keep growing, to build on their existing strength and to try new things. And the weak should not give up because something is too hard for them.

I find a great deal of wisdom in this sentence. If I separate the community into the strong and the weak, I divide it; if I treat everyone the same, I weaken it because all orient themselves toward the weakest link. A leader must do justice to weakness and strength simultaneously. In the first place, each of us tends to be both strong and weak at once. The strong have their weaknesses and the weak their strengths. Both need each other.

Benedict is part of a long tradition of considering the relationship between the strong and the weak in a community. The strong are supposed to support the weak. The prophet Isaiah says of Jesus:

Surely he has borne our infirmities and carried our diseases. (Isaiah 53:4)

As Saint Basil the Great (d. 379) pointed out, however, this did not make Christ weak! Rather, he took upon himself our weakness and illness and healed them.

In the same way, the weak are healed through the firm perdurance and health of the strong. Bearing the weak means taking on their difficulties and carrying them away. This seems to be a high ideal that would overburden the strong. But Benedict does not want to overburden anyone. His goal, however, is that the strong do not misdirect their strength. If the strong are concerned with doing better than the weak, the contest is boring. And if the strong fight only the strong and ignore the weak altogether, there is permanent competition, tying up valuable resources of strength. Strength flows in the right direction when the strong support the weak, when they give them strength, when they communicate some of their trust and capabilities. Then the weak, too, will find joy in the work and will work within their limits as well as they can. That way, both can enjoy what the weak and the strong have built together. Over the long term, this becomes a blessing for the community.

We should discern in ourselves what is strong and what is weak, and we should make peace with both sides. If we see only our strengths, we split off our weaknesses—and what we split off from ourselves, we project onto others. This creates ever more division around us. I know department heads who, wherever they happen to be working, soon divide their entire department. Because they themselves are divided, they can produce only division. Some believe that to be leadership, because it shows who is strong and who is weak, who works for the boss and who is critical. But to Benedict, this division is the opposite of leadership. Leadership means doing justice to everyone, communicating joy in the community and in work to everyone, giving everyone the feeling that they are individually valuable and needed.

If a company keeps only its workhorses and lets all weaker workers go, that may lead to short-term success. But it will soon create a climate of fear, as no one is allowed to show weakness. Every strong person has weaknesses as well. Anyone may become depressed, or have a crisis because their marriage is unstable, or become ill, or be worried about their children. In a company that kicks out those who are weak, every worker lives in fear that they might be next. No one can be strong forever. The fear of being the next to slip below management expectations paralyzes the workers and cuts them off from their actual strength.

I can show true strength only if I allow myself to be weak as well. For this reason, leadership must see it as a duty to support employees who do not correspond to expectations. This does not mean letting them do just as they please. They should still be challenged. But they should not be discouraged.

A co-worker—a person who works with the others—has the right to be supported. In such a climate, the so-called "weak" can make good on their strengths as well. And sometimes it is precisely those strengths that become a blessing to the company.

SELF-CARE

A leader should care not only for the community and its individual members—the strong just as much as the weak—but also for himself. Only then can he do justice to others. For this reason, Benedict closes the chapter on the cellarer as follows:

> If the community is large, the cellarer must receive the assistance of helpers whose support will make the burden of this office tolerable. (*Rule*, 31:17)

RATIONING ONE'S STRENGTH

In order to take on responsibility for others, I must also handle my own strength responsibly. If I am constantly overburdening myself, I will not truly help the community. I will subconsciously demand more of the community than it is capable of giving.

If I sacrifice myself completely for others, I will subconsciously link this sacrifice with expectations. I may, for example, expect others to thank me or to be just as self-sacrificing. If the community does not fulfill these expectations, I will become bitter. My work will become a constant reproach to the community and seek to produce guilt in its members. But this does not really serve the community. Guilt pushes us down and creates a climate of paralysis. I often see managers work a great deal without taking care of their own health. But at the same time, they are often very sensitive to criticism. They react harshly to any criticism: "You try working as hard as I am, then I'll listen to your opinion." It becomes clear that they do not work so hard because they enjoy it, but in order to hide behind their work and make themselves unassailable. A boss who one cannot criticize is not a superior. He is not leading but hiding behind a wall of work and sensitivity.

WITHOUT WORKAHOLISM

Working a great deal is not only a virtue. It can also be a sign of workaholism. Many managers are workaholics. They understand themselves as performance machines and are ruled by obsessions. At some point, the addictive nature of their work becomes evident, and they may either fall into drug or alcohol abuse or suffer a complete burnout. Workaholics have much that they repress. Their longing for life and love is banished to the shadows. They are cut off from their humanity, working hard in the office and allowing themselves a little bit of humanity only once they get home. This creates tension between their two personalities, which can never meet, just like the different personalities of Dr. Jekyll and Mr. Hyde in

Robert Louis Stevenson's novel. Dr. Jekyll is a kind, intelligent scientist by day, but turns into the violent, uncontrolled Mr. Hyde at night.

The more one-sidedly a person works for their company, the more dangerous their repressed shadow becomes. They will not notice the destructive aggression building up behind their supposed virtue. This aggression may then find itself expressed in the family at home, which is bad enough. But soon, it will start to affect the work as well, so that the work becomes no longer constructive, but destructive.

EQUANIMITY—CALM OF THE SOUL

Benedict intends for the cellarer to have enough co-workers that he can fulfills his duties without losing the peace of his soul. The Latin word used for these assistants is *solacia*, comforters, who aid the cellarer in performing his many duties. This Latin word literally means that a person is not left alone in their need. The cellarer should not be forced to work on his own but should have coworkers who help him bear the responsibility, with whom he can discuss how best to secure the monastery's economic future. Benedict is envisioning a team made up of members who mutually support one another. He is not thinking of the cellarer's lone decisions, but of a joint development of solutions that are good for everyone. The help of this team is supposed to enable the cellarer to complete his work *aequo animo*, with a calm or even spirit.

This term, which is the origin of the English word "equanimity," comes from Stoic philosophy, and means that a person should live serenely, free of affect and desires. A person, according to this school, should not be shaken up by extreme emotion, but should retain an inner calm through all things. To the Stoics, this is a high ideal that individuals should aspire to in every facet of their life. But Benedict understands that it is not only personal maturity that determines equanimity, but external circumstances, as well. He does not want to overburden the cellarer. Through his *solacia*, his comforters, he wants to provide the cellarer with the kind of circumstances in which he can complete his work in a relaxed way, filled with inner peace. Only then will he be able to spread peace throughout the community.

The expression *aequo animo* makes clear that Benedict cares about the cellarer and all those who have responsibility. He may repeatedly exhort them on their responsibility for their charges, but he does not want to overburden those responsible, either. The cellarer should be able to work in complete serenity and consistency.

Benedict knows that a stressed, hasty cellarer is of no use to anyone, that he will spread restlessness and haste around him. Only if a cellarer can work serenely, with inner peace, will he create an atmosphere of tranquility and peace around him. This equanimity is also a question of balance. The leader must hold his own contradictions—love and aggression, discipline and laxity, work and play, consistency and individuality—in a healthy balance. Only then can the workplace develop a balanced climate in which all employees can live their own contradictions without needing to push one aspect into the shadows. A person who is unbalanced, who lives out only one aspect of their personality, will spread a deep shadow around themselves. This shadow will envelop their co-workers in a fog of uncertainty.

THE PURITY OF THE HEART

In order to achieve inner peace, the cellarer must walk the spiritual path inward. In the Stoics' view, equanimity can only be attained by properly dealing with our emotions, by quieting the passions within us.

The original Greek word of which *aequo animo* is the Latin translation is *euthymein*. It means to be of good cheer, to be well in one's spirit, to be in a good emotional place. A person in such a state deals with his or her emotions well, allowing them, feeling them, but not being controlled by them.

To the monks, *apatheia* (detachment from one's passion), or *puritas cordis* (purity of the heart), is the state most similar to Stoic equanimity. The Desert

Father Evagrius Ponticus described the struggle for *apatheia* in great detail. The monk must become aware of his passions and must utilize the strength within them for his progress toward God. If he does so, he will achieve a state of inner peace in which he is no longer ruled by the passions, but they come to rest in him and serve him. The Desert Father John Cassian, whose writings Benedict recommends and whom he refers to repeatedly, saw purity of the heart as a state of inner authenticity in which our intentions are no longer polluted by second thoughts, in which we act out of pure love because we are open to God.

Benedict, accordingly, sets as a condition that the cellarer consistently walk the spiritual path in order to achieve purity of the heart and thus be able to lead the community with inner peace. The cellarer must not be unbalanced by the everyday conflicts between fellow monks. Only in this way can the emotional turbulence that comes from collaboration be calmed consistently. Without this inner equanimity, the cellarer would become a cause of chaos rather than a problem-solver.

AN INNER SPACE OF SILENCE

One path toward inner peace is contemplation, as Evagrius Ponticus describes it in his *Praktikos*. In contemplation, the monk finds an inner space of quiet, an inner place of God, where God himself lives in us. Neither inner nor outer turbulence can touch us in this space.

For this reason, I find it important to imagine, every morning during meditation, how the prayer of the heart leads me into this inner place of quiet, in which the triune God lives in me with all his love and forgiveness. In this inner place of silence, people's expectations and demands cannot reach me. There I find peace from conflicts and disagreements. I cannot be hurt there. In that space, I experience a healing distance from all the things that occur around me. I experience freedom from others' power, from the force of their expectations, demands, judgments, and criticisms. Only if I inhabit this inner space can I react calmly and with inner freedom to those daily conflicts.

If, however, I let myself be drawn into these conflicts too much, I cannot see through them and react to them appropriately. I will make a biased decision. But if I am in contact with my inner center through daily meditation, I will have that space within me that is untouched by day-to-day arguments, a space that does not belong to this world and cannot be ruled by worldly business.

My connection to this inner space gives me peace, relaxation, and a healthy distance from which I can react more objectively. If I am ruled by these conflicts, I will feel paralyzed and spent. I will feel that I am tilting at windmills. As soon as one conflict is over, the next has already begun. By being in contact with my inner space, I feel free to react without spending all of my energy. I have a healthy distance to matters.

Something is inside me that remains untouched by the world. I recognize personally that the task of leadership can succeed only if I consistently walk my spiritual path and am in contact with my inner space of silence while I work. Only out of this inner peace will I be able to spread peace around me. And if I am in contact with this silence, I will be less susceptible to burnout—because I can sense that this space offers a well-spring that never runs dry because it comes from God.

I can keep drawing from this well-spring, but its waters will never be spent. A person who is exhausted or spent shows that they are working out of their own strength, and not out of the inexhaustible divine source within them.

THE GOAL OF LEADERSHIP—
A SPIRITUAL WORKPLACE

In the last sentence of the chapter on the cellarer, Benedict indicates what to him the goal of leadership must be. It is the complete opposite of what leadership seminars tell us—but perhaps for that very reason, Benedict's words are a challenge for our time, as well. He writes:

> There will, of course, be appropriate times for the cellarer to hand out what is needed and for requests for goods or services to be made; these times should be observed by all so that failure to respect them may not cause any disturbance or unhappiness in the house of God. (*Rule*, 31:18f)

THE APPROPRIATE TIME

The first goal of leadership is to create a reliable, clear workplace environment. Benedict refers to the *horis competentibus*, the appropriate times, the right moment for giving and demanding. At root, *competere* means to seek to achieve something together, to come together, to be appropriate, seemly, fitting. The goal of leadership is that colleagues should seek to achieve something together. Instead of every man for himself, the goal is to create togetherness. But this togetherness should not be limited to the relationships among people, but also to the relationship between people and time, in the end between people and the creation.

The individual and their time should come together, should correspond to one another. When a person has everything in the right time, it does them good. The right time—the moment where one gets what one needs and can ask for what is needful—creates a calm, undisturbed workplace environment. When things happen at their appropriate time, every person feels they are being taken seriously. If things are in order, it helps others find their inner order.

In the ancient Greek pantheon, the *horai* were the goddesses who speeded the year and ensured fruitful harvests. Hesiod described the three *horai* as Order, Justice, and Peace, three daughters of the god Zeus. Benedict, still in the tradition of Greek culture, saw the appropriate time as not only a question of punctuality and self-discipline. Instead, Hellenic culture still had a sense of the mystery of the appropriate time, which gives human beings inner order and fills them with true rhythm. Only a person who is in touch with their inner rhythm (nowadays we would speak of their "biological rhythm") can be fruitful in the long run. None of us can work against nature and our own rhythm. Doing so is destructive. Time and individual must come together for lasting, effective, and meaningful work to occur. If a person works "by the clock," ignoring their inner clock, they will soon become exhausted and spent. Many of today's companies who have instituted a flexible time schedule for their workers have discovered this.

WORKING ENVIRONMENT

Benedict indicates the true goal of leadership when he says that nothing should cause any disturbance or unhappiness in the house of God—*ut nemo perturbetur neque contristetur in domo Dei*. This is a radically different goal from profit maximization. Benedict is concerned with the human being and human welfare on the one hand and with God on the other. Leadership should mediate, so that no worker is driven to confusion or restlessness, is disturbed or upset (*perturbetur*). Leadership should spread not haste and restlessness, but peace and clarity, serenity and joy in work. A person who drives others to haste hurts and hates them. The cellarer must not hate but love his brothers. It is an expression of his love that he creates for his brothers, not haste, but a calm and pleasant working environment in which they can enjoy working and can fulfill their tasks with inner mindfulness and equanimity.

Some businesses replace this clarity with bustling haste. New measures are announced every few weeks, and the entire company is restructured on a yearly schedule, all with the goal of being on the cutting edge of new developments. But this busy activity is only masking the fact that one has lost sight of the company's goal. This is precisely what Mark Twain was satirizing when he famously wrote:

> Having lost sight of our goals, we redouble our efforts.

The monks should always have their eyes on their goal. Then they will be able to work consistently and with inner calm. No one should be disturbed or made unhappy by leadership, no one should be driven to sadness. This sadness would only paralyze workers.

There are some companies that give the impression of a deep sadness underlying their busy activity. This sadness prevents joy in one's work—and when one looks at it more closely, it often originates in a lack of care for the individual. When people are repeatedly hurt and cannot defend themselves, they react by retreating into sadness, into depression. The normal reaction to the hurts and insults of leaders is to avenge oneself by working against one another. In this way, everyone hurts everyone, but no one speaks about it. The wounds are never examined or treated, and so keep spreading. This destroys the climate of the workplace.

In many companies, one instantly feels what atmosphere rules them. Entering the office building through its front doors, one can practically smell the atmosphere. In some cases, it is nourishing, inspiring. In others, it is oppressive, and one immediately has a queasy feeling in the stomach. These are companies in which a deep sadness is paralyzing the employees. And the entire house is shaped by a feeling of emptiness and pointlessness.

It is extremely important to Benedict that no one be hurt or unnecessarily plunged into sadness. Instead, the cellarer is to spread a climate of peace and inner joy. But this cannot be achieved through slogans or buzzwords, as was common in the Third Reich's movement of "Strength through Joy" and the like. True joy in work is only communicated by the care and respect awarded each individual employee both in encounters and through leadership style. The leader himself must never let himself be paralyzed by problems but solve them out of his inner equanimity and assurance.

A HOUSE OF GOD

Leadership should not cause disturbance or unhappiness. It should lift up and build up—specifically, build up the "House of God" in which monks can seek God together. Leadership, then, always has a spiritual task. It is supposed to build a climate in which God becomes tangible. If the monks use their eight hours of work to make life difficult for one another, if they work against one another instead of together, the three hours of communal prayer will be of no use to them in their search for God. They will block each other and themselves so completely through their work that they will be incapable of devoting themselves to God fully in their prayers. Appropriate leadership of their work areas, clear organization, a reliable flow of information, and a climate in which the individual is respected and taken seriously: these factors form the basis of lively God-seeking and true prayer.

Only if the cellarer is in touch with his own inner House of God will he be able, through leadership, to create an external House of God. This will be a place where everything tells of God: the clear order, the appropriate time, and the climate of respect and care. The cellarer's leadership task of building a House of God seems very pious compared to normal goals of business management. But the image of a House of God can be translated into our world: to create a corporate culture in which a sense of the transcendent shines through, in which the goal is higher than simple profit maximization.

If the company is supposed to mirror aspects of the House of God, that might mean, for example, that everything has its order, that the creation is seen and respected as creation, and that people are recognized as creatures of God, with all the dignity that entails. When people are respected as human beings, instead of merely as employees or performance machines, a company shows that it uses other yardsticks than utility and profitability.

Of course, being a House of God does not mean that all members of the organization have to be pious and meditate together or show their faith in God. It simply means that everything is valued appropriately, that the creation is treated respectfully, and that human beings are allowed to be full human beings. Today's employees are not satisfied with merely making money. They long for a convincing corporate culture. One beautiful image for such a corporate culture capable of attracting motivated employees might be such a House of God.

In such a House, everything is treated as a sacred altar vessel, in other words: the little things are recognized as important. Rooms are styled tastefully. Flowers remind employees of the beauty of creation. Each person's individual dignity is recognized and valued, and their non-professional interests are encouraged as well. Questions going beyond the narrow horizons of job purview are welcomed. There is room for culture, for philosophical discussion. The meaning of life is interrogated. No one is forced to commit to a creed, but the way in which people interact shows that, in the end, faith in God is the true basis of actions and behavior. And we recognize that the House of God extends beyond the company. Instead, such a corporate culture wants to affect society in a positive way, recognizing its responsibility for the entire "house" of creation.

It is interesting to see that Benedict's House of God is making a comeback with today's management consultants. I have already mentioned that Lance Secretan speaks of leaders creating a sanctuary, by which he means a space that nourishes the soul, a creative corporate culture, a company in which "spontaneity, dynamism, fun, humor, freedom from fear of failure, incentives, sympathetic values" and civility shape the workplace:

> Not so much a place, but a state of mind in which [souls] may flourish. ... Sanctuaries are led and populated by people who have made personal breakthroughs and are liberating and being liberated by their souls. (Secretan, 37f)

Sanctuaries put not profit, but people first. They do not use control, but rather ask the essential questions that move the human heart. They do not preach competition, but the unity of all human beings with one another and the unity of humanity with all of creation.

Secretan contrasts this idea of sanctuaries with mechanical organizations that operate like machines, uncaring of the soul of their employees. Such organizations create only frustration, bitterness, emptiness, meaninglessness, and sadness. The climate created by these organizations does not just affect the internal corporate culture, but it also has outward consequences. Business is probably a country's most powerful force. It creates the largest number of problems, such as for the environment, but also for the climate of society. By ensuring a humane corporate culture, business could make a significant contribution to healing society. Not for nothing did the culture within Benedictine monasteries shape medieval society and exert a healing influence on the entire country.

A company that thinks only of itself and seeks only to maximize its profits will create selfishness and profit-driven thinking in society at large, as well. Only if a company steps out of this unimaginative way of thinking and creates a humane corporate culture—a sanctuary or House of God—will it have a positive impact on society. We must move beyond mere zero-sum games in which one person wins and another inevitably loses. That way, a community can grow in which everyone wins and feels valued as an individual human being. Secretan says:

> Business has done more to integrate culture and values on our planet than organized religion or government. (Secretan, 39)

Many of today's businesses, however, are unaware of their responsibility for society. They are navel-gazing. But to me, leadership means looking beyond the narrow confines of my own organization and considering the kinds of consequences corporate culture and business practices have on society and politics. Through a Christian culture of togetherness, an organization can send a more powerful message than pious slogans that fail to reflect the realities of everyday interaction.

SHAPED BY VISION

A healthy corporate culture is shaped by vision. Such a corporate culture must look beyond its organization and have a vision of community, of working together, of the purpose and meaning of togetherness. A person who only ever reacts to the day-to-day problems will never motivate others or create significant change. In order to make things happen in the world, there must be a vision. A vision can motivate, can awaken new strength in employees. It can give one the feeling of collaborating in an important project, of making a meaningful contribution to the humanization of the world. A vision creates togetherness. It keeps the different personalities and skills of workers together, and it orients actions and behavior.

The vision must be shaped by ethical and religious values, or else it will not do justice to the individual human being. A vision needs role models for the members of its organization. And the vision must then be translated into the concrete encounters and work within the organization. Concrete goals must be established that can help realize the vision. In the words of the German poet Christian Morgenstern:

> One who does not know the goal will never find the way.

A company working without such a vision may have short-term successes. But problems will develop sooner rather than later. On the other hand, leaders who can inspire their employees with a persuasive vision, who create a sanctuary that nourishes the soul, will always speak to people's needs and will find their company flourishing.

According to Secretan, building a sanctuary requires asking the right questions. In these questions, Secretan uses terms that might be lifted straight from St. Benedict's *Rule*: He speaks of devotion and kindliness as decisive values that a manager must embody. Some of the questions are,

> Is what I do good for people? Is it truthful? Does it respect the soul? Is it courageous? Does it have grace? Does it honor male and female energies? Does it meet the needs of the personalities and souls of others? Is my energy positive? Do I respect the sacredness of other people and things? (Secretan 239)

The sanctuary, the House of God, should be shaped not by fear, but in the end by love. Therefore,

the most important questions for the manager to
ask are these:

> Do I encourage love instead of creating fear?
> Do my actions inspire joy and healing instead
> of hostility and competition? Do I win without
> creating losers? (Secretan, 240)

Most of today's managers would find it strange
to ask themselves these questions. But the future
will depend on asking just such questions. As I read
them, I felt affirmed in my own thinking. I realized
that Benedict's principles of leadership are just as
relevant today as they were 1500 years ago, and that
they could contribute to healing today's society in a
way similar to that with which they spread healing
throughout the entire Middle Ages.

CONCLUSION

Some readers may be surprised that this book has contained so few practical tips for leadership. But there are already many books with instructions and practical exercises for how to give criticism or praise, how to analyze companies' performance, or how to change management strategies from the top. There are competent consultants who teach precisely that kind of experience, and I do not want to enter into competition with them. Instead, I have consciously chosen to limit my book to the *Rule of St. Benedict*, in particular to the chapter on the cellarer and (to a lesser extent) the chapter on the abbot. But I hope that reflection on these few verses from that monastic treatise can help many who carry some form of responsibility and lead others in their work.

The challenge of those verses, first of all, is to begin with oneself: to engage with one's own passions, to recognize one's own shadows and integrate them, to practice new attitudes and learn to be at peace with oneself. That challenge means walking a spiritual path, discovering a space within oneself through prayer and meditation, and seeing how that inner space can be a source of peace for one's surroundings. These are necessary preconditions for attending to the specific tasks of leadership.

The Benedictine phrase *ora et labora*—pray and work—means that even the apparently worldly, secular tasks of leadership have a spiritual dimension. Indeed, leadership itself is a spiritual task. In that context, I understand leadership on the one hand as a sacred path, along which, through prayer and meditation I give God ever greater space within me. On the other hand, spirituality is simultaneously the trace of being alive.

Benedict requires the monk to seek God all his life. The search for God is always also the search for ever greater aliveness. God is life itself. Wherever life flourishes, there God is. For this reason, I have always considered spirituality to also mean creativity, imagination, liveliness, and joy in life. Spirituality, after all, comes from *spiritus*, the spirit. The spirit of God, the Holy Spirit, is a fount of life, the creative spirit making new things in us, making things happen in us, ensouling and nourishing us. Leadership as a spiritual task, then, is the ability to let oneself be inspired by the Holy Spirit and address problems creatively. And leadership means awakening life in others, coaxing out the life that God has imagined in them. It means bringing to fruition in others all that potential and ability that God has given them. A person who leads in this way is truly serving others, and Benedict says of such leaders:

Those who give good service to others earn for themselves a good reputation. (*Rule*, 31:8)

Leadership is an art that demands much of people. But it is also an art that can be joyful, for there is nothing better than to serve life and to awaken life in others. The thoughts in this book aim to help you discover the joy of leadership in any situations in which you lead or are led. If you can awaken life, then where you live, awakening and resurrection will become possible.

BIBLIOGRAPHY

Grün, Anselm, "Die Erzieherweisheit Sankt Benedikts:
    Vortrag beim Lehrertag am 11.7.1980 in
    Münsterschwarzach." ("St. Benedict's Educational
    Wisdom: Lecture at the Educators' Conference
    on July 11, 1980, in Münsterschwarzach.) Self-
    published. (Translator's note: Since no English edition
    of this text is available, all quotations from the lecture
    have been translated as given in the German edition
    of this volume. Page numbers, accordingly, refer to
    the German edition, and are taken from Grün's text.)

Küng, Hans. *A Global Ethic for Global Politics and
    Economics*, translated by John Bowden. New York:
    Oxford University Press, 1998.

Noppeney, Hanns G. "Führungsqualitäten 2000: Vortrag
    vor Führungskräften am 13.6.1995." ["Leadership
    traits 2000. Lecture to managers on June 13, 1995"],
    self-published, 1995. (Translator's note: Since no
    English edition of this text is available, all quotations
    from Noppeney's work have been translated from
    the German given in Anselm Grün's original text,
    rather than from the German original. Page numbers,
    accordingly, refer to the German edition, and are
    taken from Anselm Grün's text.)

O'Neill, John R. "The dark side of success," in *Meeting the
    Shadow: The Hidden Power of the Dark Side of Human
    Nature*, eds. Connie Zweig and Jeremiah Abrams.
    New York: Tarcher/Penguin, 1991, 107–110.

Reuter, Edzard. *Schein und Wirklichkeit: Erinnerungen.
[Appearances and Reality: Reminiscences].* Berlin:
Siedler, 1998. (Translator's note: Since no English
edition of this text is available, all quotations from
Reuter's work have been translated from the German
given in Grün's original text, rather than from the
German original. Page numbers, accordingly, refer to
the German edition, and are taken from Grün's text.)

Saint Benedict's Rule, translated by Patrick Barry, OSB.
Mahwah, NJ: HiddenSpring, 2004.

Schürmeyer, Fritz J. *Management-Training: Persönlichkeits-
Entwicklung – Organisations-Entwicklung.* [Management
Training: Personality Development—Organizational
Development.] Self-published, no date. (Translator's
note: Since no English edition of this text is available,
all quotations from Schürmeyer's work have been
translated from the German given in Anselm Grün's
original text, rather than from the German original.
Page numbers, accordingly, refer to the German
edition, and are taken from Anselm Grün's text.)

Secretan, Lance H. K. *Reclaiming Higher Ground: Creating
Organizations that Inspire the Soul.* Alton, Ontario
(Canada): The Secretan Center, 1997.

ABOUT PARACLETE PRESS

Paraclete Press is the publishing arm of the Cape Cod Benedictine community, the Community of Jesus. Presenting a full expression of Christian belief and practice, we reflect the ecumenical charism of the Community and its dedication to sacred music, the fine arts, and the written word.

Learn more about us at our website:
www.paracletepress.com
or phone us toll-free at
1.800.451.5006

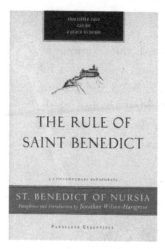